Seb's Search

MARY WEEKS MILLARD

DayOne

England and central Africa—two places of such contrast. Seb's Secret *plays out in both the quiet Herefordshire village of Gorsley and in the heart of Uganda. Abandoned as a baby under a bush in Brixton, South London, Ssebo has a personal story of sadness and tragedy; and yet it is a story redeemed by God. As one who, like Mary, has spent years living in Africa, I found her knowledge of Ugandan life and African culture a moving reminder of the life of poverty that millions face on that beautiful continent. This is the story of a hope renewed and a life redeemed.*

Mrs Alison Wileman, retired primary school teacher and a pastor's wife

© Day One Publications 2021

First printed 2021

ISBN 978-1-84625-684-4

Unless otherwise indicated, Scripture quotations in this publication are taken from the Holy Bible, New International Version (NIV), copyright © 1973, 1978, 1984, 2011 by International Bible Society. Used by permission of Hodder & Stoughton Publishers, A member of the Hodder Headline Group. All rights reserved. "NIV" is a registered trademark of International Bible Society. UK trademark number 1448790.

British Library Cataloguing in Publication Data available

This is a work of fiction. Names, characters, events and incidents are the products of the author's imagination. Any resemblance to actual persons, living or dead, or actual events is purely coincidental.

Published by Day One Publications
Ryelands Road, Leominster, HR6 8NZ

TEL 01568 613 740
FAX 01568 611 473

email—sales@dayone.co.uk

UK web site—www.dayone.co.uk

All rights reserved

No part of this publication may be reproduced, or stored in a retrieval system, or transmitted, in any form or by any means, mechanical, electronic, photocopying, recording or otherwise, without the prior permission of Day One Publications.

Cover design by Kathryn Chedgzoy

Printed by 4Edge

Dedication

To my amazing families in Uganda—
Kabanda and Florence, Emmy and Sarah,
Grace and Tomsin.
Thank you for all the joy you have brought into my life and the privilege of being part of your families.

Acknowledgements

My grateful thanks to the publishing team at DayOne for their editing and advice and for all their encouragement throughout the years.

My thanks to my friends who are willing to read my stories long before they get to a publisher, giving their suggestions and advice.

I want to thank my young friends who encourage me by asking when the next story will be published.

As always, my thanks must go to my patient husband, always encouraging me when I am writing, and never grumbling if meals are not on time!

- Chapter one -

Seb woke with a start. He was sweating with fear and shaking all over. His instant reaction was to scream, but he suppressed this by covering his mouth with his duvet. When he was younger, he used to allow the scream to emerge and his mum would come running to comfort him, but since he had gone to the senior school, he tried with all his might to be brave and not cry out.

Above his bed was a small light, and he reached for the pull cord to put it on. The darkness dispelled and he began to breathe deeply in the way his counsellor had taught him. It took time, but he had found that it did help and gradually the shaking stopped as he relaxed.

If only these nightmares would stop! Seb couldn't remember a time without them, and he didn't know why they came or what they were about. He just knew that he was somewhere that was pitch black, without windows or doors, and he had no way of escape. When the darkness became so thick and intense, threatening to suffocate him, he would wake up, covered in sweat and shaking all over. There was a smell, too. He was unable to describe it accurately to anyone; it was peculiar and only associated with the nightmare.

As Seb emerged from the nightmare, he longed to have his mum or his dad come and put their arms around him and

Seb's Search

reassure him, but he kept telling himself that he had to be brave—he was the 'big' brother. His mum had suggested that he always leave the night light on when he went to bed, but he didn't want to appear a wimp, for his sisters had long ago given up having night lights in their room.

Perhaps what worried him most was not knowing why these awful dreams came to him—always the same—the same smell, the same dense darkness and the same fear. He knew he had a different background to his sisters, for he'd been adopted when he was a few months old and had a Ugandan name—Ssebo. His skin was dark and his hair black with wiry, tight curls, which were shaved close to his head. Most people assumed his name 'Seb' was short for Sebastian, and he rarely bothered to explain.

All he had from his past was a very large shoebox. His parents had lovingly told him many times how they had longed for a baby so much, but even with help from the best doctors around, Mum had not managed to get pregnant. At that time, his parents were living in Brixton, South London. It was a noisy, busy place, with people rushing everywhere and lots of traffic. His mum told him how she went to the street markets to get most of her shopping and loved it, as they lived in a tiny basement flat which made her feel shut in, especially in summer.

He loved to hear the story of the morning when his dad was leaving for work and after shutting the door and starting to climb the steps from the basement entrance to the front gate, he heard a crying sound. He thought there must be a kitten mewing somewhere, then saw a huge shoebox almost hidden underneath

Seb's Search

a laurel bush. He was rather surprised, so he picked it up and opened the box and found a baby!

Of course, his mum and dad contacted the police, who took him to the local hospital. Nobody knew who the mother was, and even though appeals for her to go to the hospital were sent out on TV and the radio, she did not come. As soon as he was strong enough, Seb was taken from the hospital to a foster home.

His future parents had already applied to adopt a child and had fallen in love with him from the moment they set eyes on him, so even though it was most unusual to place a child in a home from a different ethnic background, they were allowed to adopt him. His mum always told Seb that he was sent especially to them, that was why he was placed by their steps!

In the box along with the baby had been a piece of paper on which was written, 'Ssebo of Mbarara, Uganda', and a blue baby grow which he'd been wearing. He now had the very large shoebox on his shelf, inside of which was the baby grow and the note, along with photos taken by the police of the box under the bush and cuttings from the local paper. That was his history—all of it.

His parents treasured him, and he loved them dearly. His dad had tried to make enquiries about his origins, particularly in Mbarara—but it had been fruitless. Mbarara was a large city—the second largest in Uganda—and they couldn't find out anything. The shoebox was British, with a picture of size seven long boots on the outside—a common make—and as the shoe firm had said when contacted, thousands of that type of boot had

Seb's Search

been sold in London alone. Seb had been found on 11 February, so that was given to him as a birthdate.

When Seb had passed his second birthday, the family moved to the country, to a small village in Herefordshire. It was an exciting time because another miracle had occurred—his mother was expecting triplets!

– Chapter two –

It was such a delightful surprise when his mum and dad learnt that the babies were expected as they had been content just to have their lovely son, but when the scan showed there were three little girls, everyone was amazed. The London basement flat was not big enough to house such a large family, and Seb's mum had always longed to return to the country, so they decided to move.

Of course, Seb was too young to remember the move from Brixton to the village of Gorsley in Herefordshire. Well, *their* house was in that county, but the boundary between Gloucestershire and Herefordshire ran right through the middle of the village—causing lots of rivalry between the families who lived in different counties! The move was such a help to Seb's parents as his mum's mother and sisters lived in the village—albeit in Gloucestershire—and so there were Grandma and aunties to help when the babies were born.

Seb's earliest memories dated back to playgroup in the village chapel and then starting at the primary school, just up the road. He was the only child with dark skin and black curly hair, but he hardly noticed that because everyone accepted him and played with him and knew him as the brother of the triplets.

Seb was thinking of all this as he relaxed with his deep-breathing exercise, and gradually the fear completely left. He fell fast asleep.

Seb's Search

A knock on his bedroom door woke him with a start.

'Wake up, sleepy head!' called his sister Rosa. 'We've all finished in the bathroom ages ago. Your breakfast is waiting!'

'OK, thanks,' he said a little grumpily. 'Just coming.'

It was a rush to get ready for school, and his head was aching. It was always the same after he had been awake in the night, but he dared not miss the school bus. The girls were waiting for him, and they rushed out of the house and up the lane to the bus stop.

'Good morning,' the driver said to them cheerfully. 'How is the Morris family today?'

'All good, thank you,' answered Rosa, who was a real chatterbox and usually the spokesperson for them all.

The bus was already half full, as it served many villages and hamlets in the area taking youngsters to the senior school. Rosa found a seat with Melody, who always seemed to have more bags than anyone else, since she was the sportswoman of the family and needed to take her kit with her every day. Elise, who was the youngest of the three girls, even if by just a few minutes, was quiet and shy and liked to sit with her brother when she could. She always seemed to know when Seb had a headache and didn't talk much on the bus. When they were nearing the small market town of Newent, she dived into her schoolbag and took out a folder and handed it to Seb.

'You left this on the hall table—I thought you needed it today,' she said.

'Oh, you are so cool! Thanks, Elise, I probably would've got a detention,' he answered. 'Then I would miss the bus home and mum would be cross with me too.'

The bus pulled into the forecourt of the school, and everyone seemed to be pushing and shoving to get off. Seb and Elise waited until the last, thanked the driver and headed to the main door.

'You ought to go and see the school nurse about those headaches,' suggested Elise quietly. 'You get just too many of them.'

'I'll think about it,' replied Seb, making his way to the Year 9 locker room. 'See you after school.'

Seb did think about it later in the day as by lunch break his head was really throbbing. He started to walk to the sickroom through seemingly endless corridors and went into the wrong room by mistake. Inside, a few kids were sitting around with books in their hands and chatting together.

'Sorry,' he muttered, realising he'd interrupted some sort of meeting. 'Is this a club? I was looking for the nurse.'

'We're the Christian Union,' a boy answered. 'You're welcome to stay. Some people call us the "God Squad". I'm Jake, by the way.'

'I'm Seb—in Year 9, but I have such a bad headache that I was trying to find the nurse.'

'She's not in today,' said a girl. 'She has Friday as her day off. Maybe we could help—we pray for each other when we're not well. Jesus made lots of sick people better.'

Seb's Search

Seb thought for a moment. 'I don't know anything much about God, but my headache is so bad, if you think Jesus can help, I'm up for it.'

'Come and sit down,' invited Jake, who seemed to be their leader, pulling up another chair into the circle. The group of kids was quiet for a few minutes, and Seb looked at them nervously. Were they up to something funny? He'd heard some of his classmates occasionally talk about the God Squad, but not in a very nice way, making fun of them as if they were weirdos.

Then Jake quietly spoke to Jesus, just as if he were right there in the room, just as he would to a mate.

'Seb here has a bad headache, Jesus. We want you to help him. Please take it away, for you are God, our great Healer. Thanks so much, Amen.'

Seb felt very warm. Maybe it was embarrassment, he thought, but most of his head felt hot, just where it had been throbbing. Then he realised that it wasn't throbbing any more. He felt fine! It was amazing!

'Wow!' Seb exclaimed. 'It's worked, your asking God has worked! The terrible headache has gone! That's so cool — thanks so much.'

'Don't thank us,' responded Jake. 'Let's thank Jesus. We can't see him, but he's alive and here with us. He healed you, not us.'

All the kids began to say aloud, 'Thank you, Jesus,' and Seb found he was saying it too, and although it seemed strange to him, he knew that this Jesus was in the room and the room seemed incredibly light, so different from the blackness of his nightmare.

The bell rang, warning the kids that in five minutes lunch break would be over and classes starting again.

'Bye, Jake,' Seb said. 'That was amazing. Thank you so much.'

'We meet here every Friday lunchtime—come and join us and learn more about Jesus with us,' Jake replied.

Maybe I will, Seb thought to himself as he walked back through the corridors to his next lesson.

The feeling of a clear head and sense of light was with him all afternoon. On the way home, Elise sat with him again.

'You look better,' she commented.

'I am. Something a bit strange but really cool happened to me at lunchtime. Maybe I'll tell you later 'cos you might understand, but I think Rosa and Melody might laugh at me.'

'It must have been something good—you look so happy now,' said Elise, as they got off the bus. 'I wonder who is at home this afternoon? Is it Auntie Apple's day?'

'Not sure. I can never remember,' Seb answered.

It was always a joke among them, not knowing who would be at home after school. When the girls were small, their mum needed a lot of help, so Grandma and the aunties took it in turn to come and help, including some of Mum's friends who were 'unofficial' aunts. This had continued all through primary school, and now that their mother had gone back to nursing at Hereford Hospital the arrangement continued as she sometimes had late shifts to work. It was fine, except for one thing—everyone called

Seb's Search

the girls 'the Triplets', and they hated that. It was as if they were lumped together as one—not three individuals who were quite different from each other, even if they looked incredibly alike.

– Chapter three –

It was Auntie Apple who greeted them at the door. The children had decided years ago to give her this nickname because she was short, quite rotund and had rosy cheeks, which somehow reminded them of a red apple. The name had stuck, and now almost everyone in the village called her by this nickname. She was very jolly and didn't mind one little bit.

'Come on in,' she welcomed them. 'I've got the kettle on. What would you like to drink?'

They ran upstairs to change out of their uniforms and then rushed into the kitchen to help make drinks and eat one of the delicious cookies still warm from the oven.

'Mmmm,' said Melody. 'You make the best cookies in the world, Auntie Apple!'

'Only one each,' laughed the older lady. 'You mustn't spoil your tea!'

'It's my turn to feed the chickens and lock them up for the night,' Seb told her. 'I'll be starving after that, so don't worry, Auntie,' and he rushed outside.

It was still quite chilly for March, and the hens were happy to go back into their coop and have some seed. Rosa, Melody and Elise helped peel the vegetables and set the table. Everyone was cheerful on Friday afternoons because there was the weekend to look forward to. Dad worked in Birmingham, but although that

Seb's Search

was quite a distance, the motorway made travel easy to Ross-on-Wye, and then it was only about five minutes on the local road, so he was normally home about 6:30 p.m.

He had only just got in and greeted everyone when they heard their mum's car come into the drive. Auntie Apple always stayed and ate with the family when she was doing 'home duty', as the children called it. They preferred to use this term as they did not want to think that people were 'babysitting' or even 'childminding' them now that they were at the senior school.

They started to talk about the weekend activities.

'I have a netball match tomorrow morning. I need to be in Ross by 10:30 a.m.,' Melody told them all. 'I'm captain this week, as Chloe is unwell.'

'I'll take you over,' her mum told her. 'I can do some shopping while you are playing. Does anyone else want to come to the shops?'

Rosa looked up eagerly and grinned. 'I'd like to, please, Mum.'

Elise shook her head. 'I'll stay here. I want to go to Kilcot Wood because I heard the daffodils are coming out and I'd like to sketch some. Our art homework is to draw some wild flowers.'

'You can't go to the woods on your own, Elise. You know the rules,' her dad said firmly.

'I'll go with you, Elise, if you like,' volunteered Seb. 'We could ride our bikes. I've got a project to finish about newts and I think there are some in the pond at Kilcot Wood.'

Seb's Search

'That's fine, then. We are sorted for tomorrow,' said Dad with a smile. 'I've promised to fix Grandma's gate—so it'll be off to Gloucestershire!'

The next day was sunny and not too cold, just right for a bike ride. As soon as the others had left for Ross-on-Wye, Elise helped Seb with the chicken coop. This was his Saturday job. The chickens were always happy to be let out in the morning and be given their breakfast. Elise collected the eggs, and then she and Seb got stuck into cleaning out the coop. It didn't take too long.

'I've left you a flask of soup and some rolls for you to take with you,' their dad called out as they came in from the garden. 'I thought as you are a bit late leaving, you might want to stay out a bit longer, but come home by 3:30 p.m.'

'Yay, Dad! That's so cool. We can have a spring picnic,' answered Elise, as she put together her sketchbook and pencils and Seb collected the things he thought he might need. They put on their anoraks and cycling helmets and were ready to set off.

As they rode side by side on the quiet road, their cheeks soon became pink as the fresh air stung them. All the family were good cyclists. As the buses were very infrequent, it helped them to get around.

They soon arrived at the woods. There was a wooden gate to go through to enter, since the woods were the property of the Forestry Commission, so they dismounted and carefully shut the gate once they were inside before cycling along the main track for

Seb's Search

a while to get near to the lake. Once there, they found a bench, took off their helmets and leant the bikes against it.

'It's so amazing here,' Elise was almost whispering. 'Just look at all the wild daffodils, and there are primroses and violets as well! I'm so glad you wanted to come, Seb—thanks.'

The wild daffodils were very small and paler than the ones in gardens and shops. They grew in clumps around the trees, some of which were also beginning to get bright green leaves after the winter months. Elise couldn't wait to start drawing.

'I've got my fishing net and jam jar, so I'll be at the edge of the lake. We must both keep each other in sight and not wander off. Make sure you have your phone in your pocket,' said Seb, trying to be the responsible big brother. 'In any case, we'll meet up at one o'clock and have lunch.'

Soon they were happily working away. Seb could hear Elise singing softly as she drew. He wondered if she'd be a famous artist one day. He was sure Melody would be a famous sportswoman. What would Rosa become? She would have to be with lots of people because she loved chatting. Perhaps she'd be a dancer; she was good at that.

As Seb dredged the edge of the pond where it wasn't too deep, he thought about himself. He loved it in the country and knew how to recognise many birds and animals. Maybe he would be a naturalist or wildlife photographer. That would be so cool!

The hour passed very quickly, and the fresh air made them hungry and soon they were back at the bench enjoying their lunch. Food always tasted nicer when they ate it outside.

'That was good of Dad to make us lunch,' Seb said. 'It's nice not to have to hurry home.'

'I'm glad you feel better. You seem really happy today,' Elise told her brother. 'I hate it when you get bad headaches—I get frightened in case something is wrong with you.'

'I did promise to tell you what happened to me yesterday,' Seb replied. 'Don't tell the others—they might make fun of me—but I know you'll understand since it was all your idea. You told me to go see the school nurse. I went in the wrong door—but as it happens, Friday is her day off. A group called the CU was having a meeting—some people make fun of them and call them the "God Squad", and I felt embarrassed. But they were really nice and when they heard about my headache, they asked if I would like them to pray for me to get better, because they believe Jesus is still alive, not someone from a history book, and he makes people well. I thought it was all a bit weird but let them do it—they spoke to him as if he were in the room and just asked him to take away the headache.' Seb paused for a moment, remembering the warmth he felt.

'And did he make you better?' asked Elise.

'Yes, that was the strange thing about it all. I sensed that someone *was* in the room with us, my head felt warm, and the room seemed full of light—I can't explain properly—but the headache was completely gone, and I've felt like I'm walking on air ever since.'

'Wow!' said Elise. 'That's awesome.'

Seb's Search

'Something inside me says that since Jesus made me better, he is alive, and I ought to learn more about him. The guys said I could join them any Friday lunchtime and I think I might.'

'Could I come too?' asked Elise. 'One girl in my tutor group is a Christian and I've always thought there was something special about her and wanted to ask her about it.'

'That would be cool if you came. We could find out things together,' answered Seb. 'Now let me see what you've been drawing, and I'll show you the two newts I caught.'

- Chapter four -

They were still sitting on the bench when a large dog appeared and rushed past them, intent, it seemed, on catching one of the ducks on the lake. It went into the water with a large splash and at first seemed to be paddling with no trouble. The duck flew off and settled further out on the lake, and it was at this point that the children noticed the dog was now in difficulty.

They heard someone running and shouting, 'Come, Rix, come!'

Out of the woods appeared an obviously very upset girl who looked to be in her teens, a lead in her hand and her hair all over the place.

The dog took no notice of the girl's command and now seemed to be struggling to keep its head above the water.

'What can I do?' she asked Seb and Elise, now crying. 'He's not my dog—he's from the rescue centre, and I can't swim. He'll drown and they'll kill me!'

'They won't do that, I'm sure,' said Elise, looking at the girl in alarm. 'Have you got a phone? Phone them and they'll come and help.'

'I can't get a signal,' sobbed the girl. 'I tried.'

'Try my phone,' Elise told her, passing it to her.

Seb's Search

Meanwhile, Seb was now worried it was the dog who might die. In his mind there was only one answer—he would have to swim out and try to rescue him.

He took off his outer clothing and ran into the lake. His dad had always told him to be careful by the lake because it was deep in the middle, but Seb knew he was quite a strong swimmer. The water was very cold, and the weeds clung around his jeans, making it hard to move his legs. It was not as easy as he thought it would be.

It seemed to Elise that it was hours before he reached the dog, but probably it was only a few minutes. She was shaking with fear as she watched Seb trying to swim.

'Don't let him die, please don't let him die!' she whispered, hoping maybe there was a God who would hear her.

Meanwhile, the girl had phoned the rescue centre, so Elise took back her phone and called her mum to come and help.

'Come on, come on, hurry up and answer,' she muttered to herself. 'Someone must be in.' It was a relief when she heard her mum's voice. Now it was Elise's turn to sob as she asked her mum to come with the car and told her what was happening.

'Take a deep breath, Elise, and explain exactly where you are, and I'll leave at once. I'll send Rosa to get Dad. Call out to Seb and tell him we're coming.'

Just as Seb had managed to get hold of the very frightened dog and turned on his back to try and swim as he had been taught in his lifesaving class, Elise tried to shout that their mum and dad were coming. Her throat had gone dry with fear, but she did her best. It gave a very tired Seb the encouragement to keep going, for the dog was big and very heavy, weighed down by his wet fur. He struggled to get away from his rescuer because he was so frightened. At first Seb tried to calm him, but then it became too much of an effort to try and talk. Once or twice he felt his own head go under the water and it was dark and cold, and he struggled to breathe as he came up.

Elise, usually so quiet and calm, was now screaming at him, telling him he was doing well and not far from the shore, and almost when he felt like giving up and letting go of the dog, he felt the bottom of the lake under his feet and knew he could make it. It took both girls to help pull the dog out and hold him still. He was shivering and shaking his fur, and Elise put her arms around him to try and calm him. The girl who had been dog walking was so shocked, she just watched.

'Take off your coat and put it round him—he's cold,' Elise told the girl, 'while I take Seb's coat to him.'

Seb had climbed up the bank, then collapsed on the grass. He wanted to get up on his feet and walk to the bench, but suddenly his legs seemed to stop working, his teeth were chattering and he felt sick. He managed to turn onto his side just before he spewed out all the contents of his lunch, plus water and weed from the lake. Elise ran down with his sweater and anorak, and even though he was wet through, she put them over him and tried to rub his back a bit to warm him up. It was such a relief when they heard the engine of a car in the distance and then saw two vehicles driving up the track through the forest.

Seb's Search

'Thank goodness you're here,' Elise sobbed to her mum, who with Melody got out of the car and rushed to help Seb. They had brought dry clothes, towels and rugs, and Elise was so glad their mum was a nurse and knew what to do.

Mum decided that Seb ought to have a check-up at the hospital since he was so cold, so she phoned for an ambulance. Meanwhile, the other car was from the dog rescue centre, and its staff were drying Rix and hearing the story of what had happened. The dog was none the worse for his adventure, the dog walker at last stopped crying and they all came over to thank Seb for his bravery.

'Thank you so much,' the centre manager was saying, but Seb wasn't in a state to respond, so his mum told the manager that she would bring Seb to the centre once he had fully recovered, then everyone could thank him, including the dog.

Dad was the next to arrive on the scene, along with Rosa, followed very quickly by the ambulance and paramedics. They checked Seb thoroughly and thought he was suffering from a mild degree of hypothermia, so he needed to go to Gloucester Hospital to be checked out. Soon he was on a stretcher, and Mum went with him. After her reassuring everyone that Seb would be fine, the others began to disperse.

Rosa and Melody rode the two bikes home and Elise rode back with Dad, who then had to do a second journey to retrieve the other car.

That evening they were all so relieved to hear that Seb was fine but would have to stay in hospital for the night as a precaution. Dad drove them all to visit him and they were pleased to see him sitting up in bed, looking his usual cheerful self.

'Are my newts OK?' he asked Elise, who told him they were fine and happy in the jam jar. She promised to put them in the garden pond in the morning.

By the time next morning came, Seb was being heralded as a hero by everyone on the ward when they heard his story. He felt very embarrassed.

'Give over,' he told the nurses and patients. 'Would you leave a dog to die if you could swim? I only did what anyone would do.'

- Chapter Five -

On Sunday morning Seb was allowed home from hospital following his adventure, none the worse for it all. However, he did want to know that Rix was alright, so that afternoon the whole family made a trip to the dog rescue centre. When Dad explained who they were, they were very warmly welcomed and Seb was thanked for his brave rescue.

'Please, can I see Rix?' he asked.

'Of course,' answered the manager. 'He's fine today. I just can't think what got into him yesterday. He's not a dog who runs off, and he has never been very keen on water either.'

The centre was quite large and there were lots of dogs, each with a large kennel and exercise area. They all looked very well cared for, and they barked at the children as if they were very happy to see them. When they reached Rix's kennel, the dog bounded over at once. The manager opened the door, and Rix rushed up to Seb. The other children were ignored!

'He knows who helped him,' said Elise in amazement.

Seb was delighted and bent down to pet Rix and tell him he was so glad he was OK. Meanwhile, Dad was talking to the manager and asking about Rix's history.

'It's interesting,' the manager said. 'He belonged to a West Indian man who very sadly had a stroke and was unable to look after him. Rix was in excellent condition when he came here;

all his injections were up to date and he was well groomed, but he's never settled very well. I think it's because our skin tone and smell are slightly different—I've never seen him make such a fuss over anyone in the way he has your son! Would Seb like to come and dog walk him sometimes? I have a feeling they have already bonded well.'

'Seb,' called his dad, 'would you like to come over here regularly and become Rix's dog walker?'

'I'd *love* that! Yes please, Dad. I've always wanted a dog, and he could be like my own dog, couldn't he?'

'I guess so, son. Before we leave, you can arrange a time to come over next week and take him out—but nowhere near ponds, please!'

The tour was a huge success, and the girls loved all the dogs too—but Rix wouldn't leave Seb's side until the manager took him back to his kennel.

'Bye, Rix,' said Seb in a comforting voice. 'I'll see you next week and we'll have a good time together.'

The arrangement worked well. Seb had a lesson in the rules about dog walking and was soon allowed to take Rix out on a regular basis. Since the evenings were getting lighter, it was easy for him to cycle to the centre almost every day after school and take Rix for a walk. Seb so enjoyed those times, and they had great fun together. He always came back and got on with his homework without any fuss. His parents were so impressed they had a talk together one evening.

Seb's Search

'Why don't we adopt Rix as a family pet?' suggested Mum. 'He would always be Seb's responsibility, but the girls would like him around, I'm sure. Also, at work I was reading about the special senses that dogs have. They can detect when children are going to have fits and things like that. Maybe he'll know when Seb is going to have one of his nightmares and the terrible headaches which follow. I'd even agree to him sleeping in the bedroom if it helped!'

'Actually, I've been thinking for a while how good it would be for us to have a dog,' said Dad, 'but I haven't said anything as this arrangement is working so well and I've been thinking of plans for the summer holidays. Could we leave adoption until after that? It would be a shame to have to send him back into the kennels so soon after our giving him a home.'

'OK,' was his wife's reply, and then they discussed the idea for the summer holiday—such an amazing one, but to be kept a secret from the children until after the Easter holidays and the girls' birthdays.

Elise and Seb started to go each Friday lunchtime to the 'God Squad' group and were surprised to find that it wasn't boring at all but fun and interesting. Everyone was friendly and made them feel part of the group, whatever school year they were in. They all shared their difficulties and worries openly, and these were prayed for, but there also was a strict rule that nothing was shared outside the group unless the person concerned was willing for that to happen.

Seb's Search

One of the other Year 7 pupils was being bullied, and after they had prayed about this, a Year 11 prefect asked if he could inform the staff, as there was a policy to investigate any bullying in the school. Seb knew that because when he had started in Year 7, he'd been bullied because of his skin colour—called some horrible names, told to go back to his own land and other unkind statements like that. When a teacher had overheard some cruel remarks, it was dealt with very quickly and hadn't recurred.

Seb had been extremely brave soon afterwards, and in a discussion time in the tutor group, he'd told them, with lots of humour, that he had been found under a laurel bush in a cardboard box—he'd even taken his precious box to school one day to show them—and everyone had laughed when he said it should have been under a gooseberry bush. That had cleared the air, and he was accepted for who he was and was now a popular boy in Year 9.

At the God Squad one day, Elise shared how she felt about always being known as one of a set of triplets and how difficult that was, much as she adored her sisters and they shared a special bond together.

'Everyone thinks we should look the same, feel the same and do the same things, because we're identical. In some ways we are sort of part of each other, but we really are very different. Rosa, who was born first, was the strongest and biggest and is very sociable and makes us all laugh, doesn't she, Seb?' She looked at her brother for confirmation. 'Then Melody is both athletic and musical, whereas I was the last to be born and was the smallest.

Seb's Search

I was born just after midnight, so technically I don't even share my birthday with the others! I much prefer doing things indoors like reading and drawing and am shy with people I don't know.

'I get angry inside when we get identical hats and scarves or jumpers from relatives for our birthday or Christmas. I want to yell and tell them that I am "me" and we are not just "the Triplets". Then I feel dreadful for thinking such things, because the family are all lovely and all help to take care of us. When we were small, they all came round to help Mum every day, and even now, if Mum is at work, there's always someone at home when we come back from school.'

The group really seemed to understand that Elise had a problem, and they prayed together about it. Then they read from the Bible a few verses from Psalm 139 that showed her that God knew all about her right from before she was born and that all of us are special and individual to him. She and Seb talked about that on the way home because the verses also helped Seb to see that the circumstances of his birth were known to God and that God had planned his birth and life too.

- Chapter six -

The following week, Rosa caused a stir around the whole school! She was a very popular girl but always getting into scrapes. It seemed unfair to her, because things just seemed to happen to her, and she certainly didn't mean to cause trouble.

Her tutor group had been doing textiles until half-term and then changed to cookery. Textiles definitely hadn't been her thing! Somehow, she eventually managed to design and sew together a felt beanie hat—and when it was her turn to put it on and parade around the class, she'd giggled as much as any of them—but inside it hurt a bit because everyone was laughing at her efforts. Thank goodness Mum didn't make her wear it and said nothing about it being a waste of money like Grandma did when she saw it. It just disappeared from sight and was never seen in the house again.

She hoped that cookery would be more fun. When she and her siblings had been small, they sometimes helped Auntie Apple, who loved to make them cookies and brownies. However, it seemed to Rosa that she had two left hands! When she broke an egg, it always seemed to land on the floor, and when she weighed out flour and then tried to tip it into a bowl, most of it somehow ended up somewhere other than where it was meant to be! Her teacher seemed to think she was doing it on

Seb's Search

purpose because she giggled a lot, but that was to cover up her embarrassment.

At the end of the lesson the previous week, Rosa had written down very carefully all the ingredients she needed for the next class. They were going to make a fruit pie, and she was looking forward to doing that and taking home something decent for the family to eat that evening.

The village of Gorsley possessed one shop. The children had nicknamed it 'Susie's Super Store' because the shopkeeper and postmistress was called 'Miss Susie' by everyone and she sold everything you could think of and would even get something in if you couldn't find what you wanted. The shop, which was the post office as well, was bang in the middle of the village, exactly where the border between the counties ran, so it belonged to both Hertfordshire and Gloucestershire.

The day before the cookery lesson, Rosa had gone to the shop with her list of ingredients and bought all the things she needed. They were put into a nice wicker basket which their Mum had bought for these lessons. The recipe had been copied and put in her file, and she went cheerfully off to school.

'We'll look forward to your pie this evening,' Mum had said as she waved them off in the morning, giving Rosa a bright smile.

All seemed to start well. Rosa read the recipe carefully, did exactly what it said, starting with putting the oven on high to get it really hot while she made the pastry. For once, the flour all seemed to go in the right place, and the pastry rolled well. She'd chosen her favourite filling, black cherries. It took a while to take the stones out of them, then cook the filling until it was a glorious sticky, sweet concoction. Rosa was pleased it hadn't burnt on the bottom of the pan, and she waited until it had cooled a bit before she put it in the pastry case and covered it with more pastry. It was looking good.

'Wow!' she said to herself. 'This is so cool! The others won't believe I've made this!'

Most of the class were way ahead of her, but Rosa had taken such care she didn't mind. She'd just miss breaktime, if necessary, to take it out of the oven.

As she opened the oven to put in her precious pie, there was an explosion and the whole oven caught fire!

Some in the class began to scream, while the teacher ran to break the fire alarm, grabbing a fire extinguisher and telling the children to walk, *not run*, to the nearest exit and assemble on the sports field as quickly and quietly as possible. The sprinklers had started to pour water from the ceiling, and the children did as they were told.

Rosa had been shocked, rooted to the ground, her pie still in her hands as if they were stuck to it, but then she made her way along with everyone else, and all the corridors were filled with people as the whole school evacuated.

Probably many thought it was just a practice fire drill, but the Year 7s who had been in the nutrition laboratory knew it was for real. Several were pale, scared and shaky, but none more so than Rosa, who was deeply shocked and still clutching her pie in both hands.

Seb's Search

The sirens of the fire engines grew louder and louder as they approached the school, and the firemen upon arriving quickly got to work. Rosa was so relieved when she saw the food and nutrition mistress come with her register and count her class. At least she was alright.

'Don't worry, Rosa', she said gently to the terrified girl. 'All is well. The sprinklers and the fire extinguisher did their job, and the fire was out before the fire brigade arrived. I'm glad it was an electric rather than a gas oven you were using.'

Once everyone was accounted for, the head announced through a loud hailer that the danger was over and would everyone please make their way into the assembly hall, starting with Year 7 groups and then continuing up to the Year 11s. Now the danger was over, it seemed as if everyone's tongues were set loose, and it was very noisy as students were trying to find out where the fire had started and what had happened. Melody and Elise were in different tutor groups to Rosa but ran over to her.

'Why have you got your pie?' asked Melody. 'You know we have to leave everything behind in a fire evacuation.'

'It was *me, my fault*. I caused the fire,' Rosa sobbed, 'and somehow the pie was still in my hands and came with me.'

Melody gently prised it out of her hands. 'Let me take it to my locker, and I'm sure whatever happened wasn't your fault. Tell us as we go to the hall.'

Relieved of her pie, Rosa began to feel less shocked and tried to tell her sisters what had happened when she opened the oven.

'I want to thank the school for being so orderly and evacuating the building quickly and quietly this morning,' said the headmaster to them all. 'It could have been so much worse if you had panicked. Year 7s who were in the food and nutrition class were especially brave, as the fire started when an oven caught fire. Miss Golding, thank you for your prompt actions, which put the fire out even before the fire brigade arrived. Obviously, that laboratory is out of action for the time being. All other classes will resume after lunch as normal. If you were in that class with Miss Golding, she will be there throughout the lunch hour and you may retrieve your belongings with her help. If you are due for a class with her this afternoon, then please report to this hall at the appropriate time and see what other arrangements have been made. Thank you all. You are dismissed.'

Rosa felt scared as she went up to get her bag and notebook—both of which were soggy. She was very subdued and tearful when Miss Golding spoke to her.

'Are you OK, Rosa? It was a terrible shock for you—what a miracle that you weren't burnt. The oven must have overheated—but that wasn't your fault. We are all just so thankful that no one has been hurt. The head would like to see you at 2:00 p.m. He is anxious to know that you are alright.'

– Chapter seven –

'Come in,' the head called after Rosa had gently knocked on the door. She was scared. She had never been called to see the head before and couldn't help feeling she must be in trouble. When she went into the room, she saw the head of Year 7 was there too.

'We are a bit worried about you,' the head said gently. 'Tell us what happened this morning. I have to put in a report, and I thought if you told us, that would be best.'

Rosa struggled to get her words out—that was very unusual for her, as she was the chatterbox of the family. She told them how she always made such a mess of things when she was trying to cook and how she really wanted to have the best pie she could possibly make to take home for her family's tea. She explained how she followed the recipe and put the oven on high while she rolled out the pastry, but it took her ages as she wanted it to be perfect. When she had opened the oven door, there was a 'whoosh' and a loud noise and flames flew out! Rosa said she was so shocked she couldn't move her hands, which were holding the pie, and she couldn't even remember how she had got into the corridor and out to the sports field.

'That's because you were suffering from shock,' the Year 7 head explained. 'Now the first thing we want you to know is that it was not your fault. The ovens are really quite old, and we know they need replacing. The school doesn't have a lot of money to do these things, but in light of what happened today I think the PTA will act.

'Shock can take quite a while to get out of your system. We've phoned your parents, and they are on their way to collect you. As your mother is a nurse, we don't feel we need to send you to the hospital, but we want you to rest this afternoon and only come in to school tomorrow if you feel your normal self. You are a sensible, good girl and sometimes accidents just happen. Go and collect your things and wait with the secretary in her office until your parents arrive.'

'Thank you,' whispered Rosa, very glad her mum and dad were on their way.

Rosa was soon home and sitting on the sofa with her mother.

'It's not often I have you all to myself,' she remarked to Mum. 'This is really cool!'

They cuddled up together, and once Rosa had related the whole story again, they decided to watch a DVD until the others came home from school.

'I know I've seen this hundreds of times, but can we watch *Anne of Green Gables* again?' she asked.

Her mum smiled. 'I hoped you'd choose that—it's one of my favourites too.'

They'd just finished watching the movie when the others arrived home, Melody carrying very carefully the pie which had caused all the trouble.

Seb's Search

'That's the most exciting day we've had at senior school,' Seb stated. 'The fire alarm went off in the middle of our maths test—so it was abandoned! Can I go and get Rix and bring him home for an hour or so?' he asked his mum, who nodded, and a few minutes later he was off to the rescue centre on his bike.

'Mum, look at Rosa's pie!' said Elise. 'It's fabulous! Can we have it for tea?'

Mum laughed. 'I'll put on the oven and we'll bake it—I'm sure it will be worth all the trouble it caused today.'

When Rix arrived, he went straight up to Rosa and started to lick her hand. Normally he was Seb's shadow, but today he seemed to know that Rosa needed comfort and sat close to her while Seb looked after the chickens.

By teatime Rosa had begun chattering to everyone again, and her mum knew she was recovering from the shock of the fire. All the family loved her pie—they didn't just say it was nice in order to cheer her up. It truly was delicious.

'Thanks for rescuing it,' she said to Melody. 'Probably it's the only surviving pie from the lesson. It should have been left in the room when we evacuated, but I don't know what happened—it was kind of stuck in my hands.'

'We are all glad it was,' remarked Seb. 'You're a really great cook to have made that. It's as good as if Mum or Auntie Apple had made it, and they are the best cooks I know!'

Rosa went pink when her brother said that—praise from him was praise indeed!

'I must rush down to Grandma's—I'll see you all in the morning,' Melody said brightly. 'She was surprised I was staying at home for tea, but I told her I just had to taste Rosa's pie after all the trouble it caused!'

Melody had sleepovers twice a week with their grandmother, who had lived in the same cottage ever since her marriage. Her next-door neighbour and great friend, Auntie Apple, had lived in her own cottage almost as long. Both ladies had been widowed for some years but enjoyed doing many activities together.

When Melody had been only six years old, she loved to sit at Grandma's piano and play the notes. Soon her grandmother began to teach her the very basics, and she showed real talent. A piano teacher had been found for her, and next to sport, music became the great love of her life. She started to have the sleepovers twice a week in order to have lots of time to practice, but her time spent with the two old ladies had developed into more than that. Melody adored them both and *loved* to hear all about the adventures they had had together as youngsters.

It had all started in the Second World War when as small girls they'd been evacuated to live in Gorsley, Grandma from Liverpool and Auntie Apple from Birmingham.

'I was terrified,' Grandma told Melody one time. 'I was billeted with a family in Gorsley who had a farm. I had never seen live cows before I arrived, and they looked so huge! I had to learn to milk them—and we did that before going to school and when we came home again. The farmer's older son and daughter tried to help me and were always laughing at my "townie" ways.

Seb's Search

Sometimes they played practical jokes on me, but it was always in fun. We all got on very well together.'

Auntie Apple had been listening and began to laugh.

'So,' she told Melody, 'your Grandma fell in love with Bill, the farmer's son, and ended up marrying him!'

Through her visits, Melody learnt all about life on the farm and the time when Elsie, whom they now knew as Auntie Apple, arrived from Birmingham and was also billeted there. By that time, Grandma was able to do lots of the farm work, and it was her turn to help teach the new 'greenie', as they called Elsie.

'It was a bit nicer for me,' Auntie Apple told Melody. 'I had an older brother who was billeted with a family just up the road at Kilcot House. That family ran a market garden, and he learnt all about plants and ended up as a gardener. Mum used to come and see us quite often because Birmingham wasn't too far away—but Liverpool was so far away that your Grandma rarely saw her mother.'

'It wasn't too bad though,' chipped in Grandma. 'I had a good time with the family at the farm, and your mum always made a fuss of me when she visited.'

Almost every time Melody had a sleepover, after she had finished her music practice, the two old ladies would tell her stories, and even though some of them she had heard many times, she still loved to hear them again and began to write some of them down in her notebook.

The cottages the elderly ladies lived in were also old. Grandma still had a scullery outside her kitchen, and there was

Seb's Search

a strange brick oven, now covered over with a board, which had once been a place where all the leftover food had been stored and then cooked up as pig's swill. In the war, Melody was told, every person in the village was encouraged to keep a pig, and the swill oven was how the food for it was made. Once it was well grown and fat, the pig would be taken to the local slaughterhouse to be prepared as meat and bacon for feeding the family throughout the winter.

'I'll never get rid of my swill oven,' declared Melody's grandmother. 'The pig was always my Bill's pride and joy; just like a pet it was, and he even shed a tear or two when the time came for slaughter. Then he'd go back the next day to his work at the farm and choose another piglet to bring down here. All the kids loved the pigs, your mum included. We kept chickens and ducks in our little garden, and of course, we were all "digging for victory", growing our own fruit and vegetables.'

That evening it was Melody's turn to tell a story to the ladies. She told them all about Rosa's pie and the oven exploding and the fire brigade coming. 'We only had the pie because Rosa was so scared that she didn't think to put it down but carried it all the way to the sports field where we had to assemble. Then I took it and put it in my locker and brought it home. All the rest of the class had soggy pies from the sprinkler—but that's why I had to stay at home for tea this evening, and it was *so* good, it would have been such a waste to have abandoned it!'

Seb's Search

Auntie Apple began to giggle. 'I didn't set the school on fire, but Jane, do you remember the time Bill switched the sugar and salt?'

Grandma grinned. 'You bet. How could I forget! It was autumn, and we had been in the orchard picking up the fallen apples. We were given cookery books by the Ministry of Agriculture and Fisheries in those days, teaching us how to cook with the food that was available. Well, I decided to make an apple crumble. I know everyone loves them these days, but it was one of the wartime recipes that had just been invented. I started rubbing the fat into the flour—very careful not to spill even the tiniest bit of flour as it was so precious. We were all in the farmhouse kitchen, and as I was doing this Bill swapped round the sugar and salt canisters. I tipped in what I thought was sugar and added it to the mixture, put it over the cut-up apples and popped it into the oven.

'It looked lovely when it was cooked, but when we tried to eat it—it was so horrible! I burst into tears and Bill went *very* red in the face, so his mum guessed he had been up to mischief. He was punished quite severely, and we all felt sorry for him, but food was precious in those days and he had wasted a lot! We have laughed about it over and over through the years. He was quite a one for pranks and mischief, was your grandfather!'

'Now before you go to bed, young lady,' Grandma said, 'your birthdays are coming up soon. We were thinking of knitting you each a lacy cardigan, seeing that hand knitting is fashionable again. Would you all like red ones?'

Melody took a deep breath. She and her sisters had often said how much they hated being given identical clothes and all looking alike, especially now they were at senior school. She didn't want to hurt these two ladies whom she adored, but it was her chance to explain something to them.

'Well, Grandma,' she said, as gently as she could, 'we were thinking only the other day, now that we are growing up into young ladies, how much we like different colours. Rosa loves red, but Elise's favourite colour is yellow—a kind of buttery colour, and my favourite colour has always been blue, especially pale blue. Do you think you could make us ones in our favourite colours? In one way they would be the same, or the pattern would be the same, but the colours would reflect our different personalities.'

'What a clever idea!' exclaimed Auntie Apple, and Grandma nodded. 'I don't know why we haven't thought of that before. Why, it would help us to tell you apart!'

Relieved, Melody gave them both a goodnight kiss and made her way up to bed.

– Chapter eight –

Just before the Easter holidays, Seb once again was having nightmares. They troubled him so much that he began to hate bedtime and made up all sorts of excuses to stay up a bit longer. His sisters guessed they were happening because he was tired and grumpy in the mornings and had dark circles around his eyes.

Several times he wondered if he ought to ask the God Squad to pray for him, but he really didn't want to share his nightmares with the whole group, especially since Elise belonged and he didn't want to worry her. Seb did think that he might tell Jake, but he rarely saw the Year 11 pupil apart from at the Christian Union meeting.

One morning, however, he was getting off the school bus and going through the main gate when he met Jake.

'How are you doing, mate?' Jake asked him. Seb was just about to answer 'Fine' when he realised that this was an opportunity to tell his friend that he had a problem.

'I have a really bad problem. Could I talk to you on your own sometime?' he asked Jake.

'Sure. Are you free this lunchtime?' his friend asked. 'I could chat then. We could meet in the prayer space—bring your packed lunch with you. I'll check that's it's free to use; if not, we'll find a corner in the dining hall.'

Seb's Search

It was good to find that the small room which the school used as a 'prayer space' was empty and the two boys could use it to talk freely. Seb told Jake the story of the terrible nightmares he'd experienced all his life and the headaches which followed. He told him how wonderful it had felt after the time the God Squad had prayed for him, the light he had seen and the lightness he felt in himself for some time afterwards, but now the dark nightmares were happening more and more frequently, and he was scared.

Jake listened to all of Seb's story and at first wasn't sure what to say or how to help. He silently prayed, and then it came into his mind. His Uncle Dave! He was the minister of the chapel at Gorsley—he would know how to help.

'Seb,' he said, 'I think your problem is too big for me, but would you let me talk to my Uncle Dave about it? He's the minister of the chapel in your village. He's very wise. I promise I won't tell anyone else in the group, but can I talk to him? I think it's a spiritual problem rather than physical, and he would help us know how to pray.'

Seb hesitated for a few moments, then agreed. Anything to get rid of the nightmares!

'OK, I'll message him this evening and get back to you,' said Jake. 'I've got your phone number, so I'll contact you as soon as he replies.'

By the time he arrived home from school, Seb had received a message to say that Jake's uncle would be glad to help, and a meeting with all three of them was arranged for the coming weekend. Jake's uncle had suggested that it would be a good idea for Seb to tell his parents about the meeting, and he agreed to do so. Seb's dad and mum only attended services on special occasions, but Auntie Apple was a staunch attender and Grandma often went along with her, so there were no objections to Seb seeking help from the pastor. His parents too were worried about Seb's nightmares, and although the counsellor he had seen had been helpful about the management of them, he had no real answers for Seb.

A very nervous Seb walked up the chapel lane on Saturday afternoon. He had taken Rix with him, just to help him keep calm. He needn't have worried. Jake's uncle was a kind guy and Seb liked him at once, and so did Rix. Jake helped him by telling his uncle what Seb had already told him.

'Let's ask God to help us,' Uncle Dave suggested and said a very simple prayer before he gave any advice.

'There's a verse in the Bible which will help us,' he told Seb and opened his Bible to the Gospel of John and chapter eight, verse twelve. 'Look what Jesus says: "I am the light of the world. Whoever follows me will never walk in darkness, but will have the light of life." When you were prayed for by the God Squad at school, not only did your headache go away, but you sensed warmth and light, right?' the pastor reminded Seb.

'Yes, I did, and it was so cool, I felt like I was walking on air for several days. Then the nightmares returned worse than ever.'

'That day, Jesus was in the room answering your prayers, because he is alive, even though we do not see him with our physical eyes. Even so, you sensed his presence and his power to heal you, bring light into the darkness you had experienced and give you joy and happiness. Jesus is the light of the world, but his enemy, and ours, Satan, is full of darkness and wants to spoil our lives, draw us into his darkness and keep us away from the light and life that Jesus wants to give us.

'One of Satan's ways to do this is to use any traumatic experience we might have had, even in the womb before we were born or in our early life, so we have no physical memory of it, and turn it into darkness. I think the nightmares that keep coming back to you are rooted in a traumatic event before or just after your birth. It could even be the darkness in the box in which you were left as a baby—but it may have been before that. That doesn't matter. What matters is that Jesus wants to take it away forever.'

Seb sat quietly, trying to take in what the pastor was saying. It made sense somehow.

'I want to have that light and warmth and happiness in my life always,' he told the pastor.

'You can—from this afternoon on,' he was told. 'There are two kingdoms, God's kingdom of light and Satan's kingdom of darkness. We are all born into the latter. That's why Jesus explains to us earlier in the Gospel of John, chapter three and verse sixteen, that we need to be born again—not as a baby, but spiritually into God's kingdom of light—and become a child in his family.

Seb's Search

'Because everyone in the world has been born into Satan's kingdom, we all do wrong things—I don't need to tell you that, I'm sure. To come into God's kingdom, we have to ask him to forgive us for all the bad things we have done, and because he loves us and sent Jesus to die for us, he will answer that prayer and we are born into his kingdom of light.'

'That makes sense,' said Seb thoughtfully. 'Did the nightmares come back because I am still in Satan's kingdom? I think I would like to be born into God's kingdom.'

Just where he was, Seb prayed from his heart, asking God's forgiveness for all the times he'd messed up in any way and asking to be born into God's family. Then the pastor and Jake prayed for him and for the nightmares to go away forever. Seb could only describe what he felt afterwards as feeling like he was a different person inside.

Jake and his uncle were so happy for him, and the pastor gave him a Bible to keep and suggested he start to read Saint John's Gospel. He also told him that there was a youth group at the chapel and that if he was able to join he would learn more, because like any baby born into a family he had to grow, and the group would help him to do that.

That night Seb read again the two verses which he had been shown by the pastor and wrote them out and put them in his shoebox—to mark his second birthday, the day he was adopted into God's family.

After that Saturday afternoon, Seb noticed a real change in his life. The nightmares stopped and never returned, and he

Seb's Search

wasn't plagued by the terrible headaches. The whole family were so happy for him, and he tried to explain to them about being a Christian and in God's family. Elise already understood a bit about that, and she started to go to the youth group at the chapel with him. They had such fun times that soon Rosa and Melody joined as well, and at Easter the whole family went to the chapel services.

'I think I'd like to continue going,' Melody told them. 'Maybe I could join the music group—the band is really cool.'

'Mum and I are thinking of going regularly too,' responded Dad, 'but it's up to you if you want to go. We will never force you.'

- Chapter Nine -

After Easter, just before the summer term started, the Morris family celebrated the triple event of the girls' birthdays. It was always a very special time, but this year they were celebrating becoming teenagers! There was going to be a big crowd—Grandma and Auntie Apple, Mum's sisters, their husbands and children, some school friends, the new friends they had made at the chapel youth group and to their great delight, their dad's parents, Grandpa and Grannie, were coming from Devon and going to stay for two weeks' holiday.

They were very much hoping the weather would be fine for the barbeque and dance which was to be held in the farmer's barn at the end of the road. He rented it out for village events and parties. The week before the party was a bit cold and showery, but it warmed up towards the weekend, and then Saturday promised to be a lovely spring day.

Everyone was up bright and early. The breakfast table was piled with cards and gifts for the girls, and there were many oohs and aahs as they opened them. Their parents had decided to give them vouchers to buy some new summer outfits.

'There's a reason for this,' their Dad told them. 'For our summer holiday, we are going to Africa!'

All the kids screamed with delight and amazement. 'Where, Dad, where?' asked Rosa.

Seb's Search

'We are going to Uganda—we decided that it was time that Seb went to visit his birth mother's native country. Even if we can't find any relatives, he should know his background. So, girls, we thought you would like to choose some clothes with that in mind. The hotel we have booked has a swimming pool, and we hope to go on safari to a game park. It will be a once-in-a-lifetime adventure for us all, so we'll make the most of it.'

'However,' said Mum, 'we'll all have to have vaccinations beforehand—so we don't want any grumbles when the time comes.'

'Oh, that is so cool! We won't make any fuss,' promised Rosa, looking at her brother and sisters, who nodded in agreement.

'Well,' said Dad, smiling at his family, 'birthdays or not, the chickens need cleaning out and then I guess you will take Rix out as usual, Seb? I could do with you girls helping me to decorate the barn. Let's give Mum a bit of space until lunchtime.'

The girls took their presents up to their rooms.

'Do you realise,' commented Elise, 'that this is the first time we have had different presents from Grandma and the aunts? Look at my gorgeous yellow cardi—I'll wear it this evening with my jeans and top. No one has given us matching red bobble hats!'

They all laughed.

'Maybe being teenagers makes a difference,' remarked Rosa. 'We're not just "the Triplets" anymore but three young ladies!'

'Hope so!' answered Melody, smiling because she'd had a hand in suggesting colours for the cardigans. 'I'm just going to

Seb's Search

message them to say thank you before we help Dad—there'll be so many people this evening that it may be hard to talk to all of them then.'

It was fun getting everything ready for the party, and the aunts arrived to help Mum with the food. As so many guests were expected, she had made three birthday cakes, one for each of the girls, with thirteen candles on each of them. Rosa had red roses on hers, Melody's was decorated with musical notes and symbols and Elise's had a palette, pencils and paints. They looked amazing!

Dad took them all out to lunch in Newent for a Chinese meal as a special treat. Then they drove into Gloucester to collect Grandpa and Grannie from the train. When they got back home, while their grandparents unpacked and rested, the children all helped to take the food to the barn and get everything ready. A local band soon arrived to set up their equipment while the children ran up the road to change into their party outfits before all the guests arrived.

'Yay!' said Seb when they all arrived back at the barn. 'This is so cool!'

Dad and the uncles were outside with the barbeque, and the rest of the food was laid out inside the barn. After everyone had enjoyed a drink and been chatting for a little while, the meal began. There were so many different things to eat, and they were all delicious.

When the band had finished eating their meal, they began to play and sing. Soon the dancing began. All the chairs were rearranged around the edge of the barn, leaving plenty of room for dancing and a good view for those who just wanted to chill out and watch. It was huge fun, with everyone from the youngest guest, who was just three years old, to the grandparents and Auntie Apple having a dance.

After a while, there was a break, during which the candles were lit on the cakes and everyone sang 'Happy Birthday' to the girls. It was quite difficult to fit in all three names into the song, and it resulted in much laughter. The girls, at a signal from their dad, blew out the candles at the same time, and once again there was much laughter as they all tried to blow them out in one breath. The cakes were then cut, and teas, coffee or cold drinks served. It was a good time for school friends to meet the youth club friends and for the grown-ups to chat.

The band struck up again for a final session of dancing which ended with some traditional country dancing.

'A real good knees-up,' Grandma called it, 'just like we had in the war when I was a teenager, only I don't think they called us that—teenagers weren't yet invented!'

Just before the end, Dad got up to thank everyone for coming and all who had worked so hard to make it such a lovely party. It all ended with three cheers for the girls, Rosa, Melody and Elise. Before they went home, many of the family and local friends helped clear up the barn, so it didn't take too long.

'That was the best party we've ever had,' Rosa told her parents when they reached home. 'Thank you so much! We've all taken lots of photos for our memory books!'

Seb's Search

It was hard to settle down at school again after all the excitement of the holidays, but exams were coming and there was revision to be done. Seb also had to choose his options for his GCSE course for the next two years. Then came the trips to the doctor's surgery to start the courses of injections ready for the trip to Uganda.

'No gain without pain!' Mum had reminded them. 'You promised me no grumbles.'

The nurse at the travel clinic was very jolly and took their minds away from the procedure by telling them funny stories of the times when she had travelled around the world as a young woman soon after qualifying as a nurse.

'One day,' she told them, 'I was on a plane on the way back from Kenya and next to me was an African bishop. He told me that he was going to an important meeting in London but had never been on a plane before. The stewardess had served our meal and then came along with coffee. She looked at the bishop and asked, "Black or white?" and he pointed to his arm and said, "Can't you see that I'm black?" She was covered with confusion, and I gently told the bishop she was asking if he wanted black or white coffee. Then he burst out laughing, and we all giggled and kept on giggling about it for most of the flight!'

The kids started to giggle too.

'Good job you don't like coffee, Seb,' remarked Melody. 'She won't ask you "black or white"!'

Rosa had made a very good friend called Sophie at the chapel youth club. They always sat together during the Sunday service as well. Sophie was in the same school year as the girls but went to a different school in Monmouth, which meant a long bus journey each day, so they rarely were able to meet up after school but were inseparable at the weekends. After one of the holiday injections, Rosa was a bit grumpy because her arm was sore and she didn't feel like doing anything energetic on Saturday, so the girls were just chilling out in Sophie's bedroom. Rosa began to tell her friend why she had needed the injection and where they were going for their summer holiday.

'Wow!' said Sophie. 'That's so cool! I have a cousin who lives in Uganda. She's a missionary and works with street kids in Kampala, the capital city. She's a lot older than me and is married to a Ugandan guy, who is a lawyer. I'll tell you what—I'll email her and tell her my best friend is going to be in Uganda for her holidays. Maybe you'll even get to meet her. She's great fun.'

'We're going to stay in the west—a big city and I can't remember the name very well. But it begins with "Mb" and ends with "ara" or something like that. It's where Seb's family came from, and Dad wants him to connect with his culture since he knows nothing about his birth parents.'

'Let's do it now,' said Sophie in excitement. She opened her laptop and booted it up. Soon she was writing to her cousin Naomi. Rosa told Sophie all she knew about the holiday and remembered that they were going to the Queen Elizabeth National Park for an outing.

A reply came back within minutes, for Naomi was at home with her computer on. She told the girls that the town would be

Seb's Search

Mbarara, that it was the second largest city in the country and that it was in the Ankole region, about five hours' drive from the capital city, Kampala.

'If your friend's family would like it, we could meet them at the airport at Entebbe and take them to Kampala. It's a bit safer than local taxis, which often drive too fast. Give my email to Rosa's parents and let them contact me, if it would help,' Naomi wrote.

That was good news, and Rosa was sure that her parents would be very pleased to have a contact like Naomi and her husband George.

Rosa had a sleepover that night at Sophie's house, and Sophie's family were also very excited to hear about the trip to Uganda and hoped that Naomi could meet up with them.

The next day, after the service at the chapel, Sophie's parents talked to Rosa's mum and dad, who were indeed very pleased to have a link person in Uganda. Suddenly, the holiday seemed more real as they received emails from Naomi and George, who not only promised to meet them when they arrived but also offered accommodation for their first night before their onward journey to Mbarara.

- Chapter ten -

The summer term passed very quickly. Rix spent a lot of time with the family, staying every weekend with them. They were all looking forward to his being adopted when they came back from Africa, and it was nice to have something special to look forward to once they came home.

After the exams were finished, school relaxed and there were events like Sports Day, at which Melody and Seb both excelled. Seb was very good at long-distance running, and Melody was good at almost every event. Her house captain was thrilled because she managed to win so many house points that they won the sports cup, and that hadn't happened for a few years!

Rosa was so popular in her year group that she was elected to be the representative for the school council when they returned in September and be a junior prefect.

Elise was very surprised when she learnt that her exam results were so good that she had been awarded a prize for the pupil who had made the most progress in Year 7. She was commended as well for her artwork.

Altogether it was a very happy ending to the school year. On the last day of term, the children couldn't wait to put their school things away and begin packing for the great holiday adventure in Uganda.

Seb's Search

Right at the end of July, the long-awaited day arrived, and the Morris family were driven by their uncle to Birmingham Airport. It was a warm, sunny day, which helped everyone get into the holiday mood.

The airport was busy, and it seemed to take ages to get through all the security checks and into the departure lounge, then finally board a small plane which was taking them to Amsterdam. Once in the plane after all the safety checks and explanations, they were soon in the sky and thrilled to be on their way.

It was the first time they had flown abroad, and so that itself was an adventure. They had some time to spend in the airport at Amsterdam, but the kids found that fun, wandering through the shops looking at all the Dutch souvenirs.

Eventually it was time to go through another lot of security checks, then board a bus to the terminal from which the Africa flight would depart. That was when the excitement really began to bubble up—soon they would be on their way to Uganda. The plane was full, but they had two rows of seats, one in front of the other, on a window side. This meant they could take turns sitting near the window until it was too dark to see anything. By then, dinner was being served. It was a new experience for all four children, and they ate everything they were served. They each had a small screen in front of them and could watch a film or just listen to music, which they did for a little while, but eventually tiredness overcame them and they settled to sleep.

Seb's Search

It seemed incredibly early in the morning when the stewardess woke them with breakfast! However, by the time they had eaten and then visited the tiny bathroom to wash and tidy up, the pilot was telling everyone to put on their seat belts and prepare for landing.

Melody was sitting by one window and Seb by the other. Elise and Rosa leaned over as far as they were able to see the landscape as they came in to land. It was so exciting to get their first glimpse of Africa. They could see little houses with tin roofs and windy red roads and a glimpse of the Lake Victoria, which was so huge it seemed like the sea.

'Aircrew, take your seats for landing,' announced the pilot over the loudspeaker. Then there were a few bumps as the wheels touched the runway, and they were down. They were in Uganda!

It took a little while for the six of them to get through the immigration area, because Dad had to buy visas. Once that was done, they went to collect their baggage, and Dad was very relieved to find that it was all there—he'd heard tales about luggage getting lost en route to Africa from some of his workmates.

Wearily they made their way with trolleys of luggage into the arrivals lounge and were so pleased to see a young woman holding up a placard which said, 'Welcome to the Morris family.'

Rosa rushed over to Naomi, with whom she had talked on Skype one day with Sophie, and gave her a hug. Her husband

Seb's Search

George was waiting there as well, and all the family were soon introduced.

As soon as they left the airport, the heat and humidity seemed to hit them. It felt so different from England, even though it was still quite early in the day. Seb felt quite emotional and struggled to blink back a few tears, though he didn't really understand why. Was it because his ancestors came from this country? George looked at him and seemed to understand.

'It's strange coming to a country which you have never visited, yet it seems like home, isn't it, Ssebo?' he said, using Seb's full name. 'You'll hear your name all the time over here, but it isn't because people know you—it's because it means "Greetings, man"! You'll get used to it. This will be very special for you, to see the place where your family came from. I hope you will take lots of photos so that one day you can show your children their heritage.'

'I will, sir,' answered Seb, swallowing down the lump he felt in his throat, then giggling a little at the thought of being grown-up, married and having children—that seemed a million miles away!

The family were so glad that they'd been met by Naomi and George, for the traffic to Kampala was fast and furious. Vans, cars, taxis and buses were racing past each other and honking their horns. Travelling along the road, they saw several rusted cars, the results of accidents, they guessed. People were also walking on the verges, and some were carrying baskets or bags on their heads. It was all so different from their quiet little village of Gorsley!

'We have left the town of Entebbe now,' explained Naomi. 'Entebbe means chair or seat, and when Uganda was a British protectorate, all the government offices were in the town, which is why it was given that name as the seat of government. It was not the best place, because it was so near to Lake Victoria that there were many mosquitoes, which caused a lot of malaria. It was better when the capital was established in Kampala, twenty miles inland.

'We will soon be at our home. We live about halfway between the two towns, at a place called Lubowa. It used to be a tea plantation many moons ago, but it's a very pleasant place to live in and so good not to be in the middle of Kampala, although that is where we both have our work.'

Soon they turned off the main road and travelled up a red dirt road.

'Close the windows,' suggested George, 'or you will find the dust coming in and covering everything. I'll put on the air conditioning, but we're nearly home.'

The house was a long bungalow, set in a pretty garden. Behind it were some small outbuildings, which they learnt about later when they explored the grounds.

Inside the bungalow it was light and airy—all the windows frames had wrought iron metal bars—and the actual windows opened inside, keeping inside cool but also giving security. There were several young people in the house, and Naomi explained

Seb's Search

that some of the street children she worked with now helped her in the house, and she was teaching them life skills. They helped to carry all the cases inside and show the family where they would sleep.

Once they were settled, it was time for brunch—a lovely meal where they all sat around a huge table. The Ugandan children were able to speak some English, since it was taught at school and was the second language for the country, but they also all spoke Luganda, the language of the local area and Baganda tribe.

'We have ten children who live here,' George told them. 'Six are at school in this village, and they will be back at 1:00 p.m., and then our four other youngsters here will go for the afternoon until 5:00 p.m. In Uganda there are so many children that most schools have two sessions.'

After brunch, George suggested that he take everyone to Kampala, where they would need to visit the British embassy and register their presence in the country, and then to the bank, where they could exchange some of their money. 'We'll park at my offices. It's safer to leave the car there. I'm afraid that neither Kampala nor Mbarara are very safe places—you need to be streetwise here. In a country where people are so poor, you will see many beggars who will keep asking for money. It is better not to give it to them, because if you do, in minutes there will be a whole crowd around you demanding money.

'If you wish to help the poor people, it is better to give something to Naomi who works with the homeless, and she'll make sure it goes towards food and not be spent on drugs or cigarettes. Be very careful with your bags, phones and cameras too. I know it's horrible not to think you are trusting people, but as well as many good people here, there are also bad ones.'

'At our home the children are all trustworthy, so you needn't worry so much, but still be sensible,' added Naomi.

It took a while to get Ugandan money, have their phones checked to make sure they worked in Uganda and then register at the embassy. It was cool at the embassy, and they were given cold drinks and biscuits.

'Thank you so much,' Elise said for them all. 'It was so hot in the centre of town, and so noisy.'

The lady who had given them the drinks laughed.

'It took me a little while to get used to all the heat and noise, but you'll grow to love this country very quickly,' she promised.

The family were also given some leaflets with advice should they have any trouble in the country at any time, especially if they hired a car and had a breakdown or any of them became sick.

After visiting the embassy, George took Dad to hire a car for their three weeks in Uganda, while Naomi took everyone else to a good bookshop to buy a road map and guidebooks.

'I just don't know how we would have managed without your help,' Mum said to Naomi. 'There are so many things we hadn't thought about when we decided to come here. Thank you so much for your kindness.'

'It's such a pleasure,' Naomi answered. 'It's lovely to meet Rosa and hear all Sophie's news and catch up with news about

Seb's Search

Gorsley. We love having visitors. We want you to come and stay a night before you leave the country—you'll need George to help you take the car back. It's so much easier when the locals realise you are not just a tourist whom they can rip off.'

Back at the bungalow, the six children who had been to morning school all made friends and took Seb and the girls around the garden. The outbuildings had been for servants when the house was built, but now they were rooms for the children who lived with Naomi and George. They were very small, with several beds in each one, but they were clean and tidy. The children had 'long drop' latrines at the back of their houses but otherwise had all their meals and showers in the main house.

'Several of us are orphans,' explained one of the older boys. 'My parents died of AIDS, and I'm HIV positive, but I keep well because Uncle and Auntie pay for me to have medicines to take, which stop me from becoming sick.'

When the Morris children heard the stories of the street kids and how they had tried to survive, they were sad. They had no idea how hard life was for kids in other countries.

'That could have been my story,' Seb said sadly. 'Who knows what would have happened to me if Dad hadn't found me under the laurel bush?'

- Chapter eleven -

Seb took a long time to get to sleep. He guessed it was the same for the girls as he could hear them talking in the next room. It had become dark at 6:00 p.m., as they were near the equator, but they had all gone to bed soon after supper. He lay under the mosquito net and listened to the humming of insects and the chattering of the children in the hut behind his room. He tossed and turned for ages, not used to the heat and humidity. Eventually he fell asleep dreaming of playing football and that all the team had the same skin colour as him and he could understand their language!

The next day it was light by 6:00 a.m., the cock was crowing and there was a lot of noise around the houses. As soon as they had showered and dressed, all the luggage was loaded into the four-wheel drive vehicle which had been hired to take them on the next stage of their adventure.

At breakfast, George asked if he could pray for a blessing on the Morris family before they travelled. He asked God to go ahead of them, protect them and give them a wonderful time. Once again, Seb felt a lump come into his throat. He was so thankful that his new friend, Jesus, was with them. It was all so exciting, but also scary, because there were so many hazards in a strange country.

Seb's Search

Everyone was a bit tense as they made their way through the capital city and on to the road leading west. The girls had been chattering, and Dad snapped at them.

'For goodness' sake! Just stop that noise for a bit, I'm trying to concentrate!'

'Sorry,' they said in unison. Seb and Mum were sitting in the front, along with Dad. They were poring over the map to make sure they found the right road out of town. Once they were on the open road, they all relaxed.

It was interesting to look at the scenery. Seb was fascinated by some of the trees, which seemed to have woven balls hanging from them. Elise looked in the guidebook and found they were nests made by weaver birds. They stopped for a few minutes to look more closely and take photos. They even saw some of the bright yellow birds flying around.

The day was getting hot, and they were glad for a break. All of them had bottles of water and needed a drink. It would have been nice to have stayed and watched the birds, but people were gathering around them mostly speaking in their own language, and some of them were bold enough to try and touch the girls' skin and fair hair. That made them a bit scared and reminded them that they must be careful of their purses and phones.

'Goodness!' their dad exclaimed. 'I don't think I locked the car. Come on, kids,' he called, 'back in the car as quick as you can!'

It was a relief to get back in, even though the kids outside were peering through the windows and some were holding out their hands asking for money.

Seb's Search

'I feel like a monkey in the zoo,' remarked Rosa. 'It's alright for you to laugh, Seb, but you have the same colour of skin and hair as they do, so they're not curious about you!'

'That's all it is,' said their mum. 'Naomi warned me that in the villages they are not used to seeing *mzungus*, as they call white people, up close. We just have to be a bit careful if we stop to take photos. She said that if we take photos of the people, some of them might demand money—but don't give them any.'

'We drive along the side of Lake Victoria for quite a long way now, and you will get some views of the lake,' their dad told them. 'Then we'll come to the equator, and that's a good place for us to stop and have a short break. It's a tourist spot and you can take plenty of photos.'

'I can't believe how huge this lake is,' remarked Melody. 'It goes on forever!'

'It's like being at the sea,' Mum said. 'They have some big ferry boats crossing over from Tanzania. It's far larger than any of the lakes we have in England.'

It was huge fun stopping at the equator. The actual place was marked by a monument in which people could stand and have their photos taken, so one by one they did that and then the whole family had one taken together. It was the first photo they posted on social media for all the family and friends to see at home. At the souvenir shop nearby, Elise bought herself a T-shirt on which was printed on the back 'I'm a Mzungu!' since she had learnt it meant 'I'm a white person.'

Seb's Search

'You can't wear one like this,' she teased Seb. 'You'll have to have a special one printed with "I'm British".'

The next stop was a town called Masaka, where they found a restaurant that served fish and chips! The fish was straight from Lake Victoria and was called tilapia, and they loved it.

'Now we are about halfway to Mbarara,' Dad told them, 'so we need to get a move on. I'd like to reach the hotel before it gets dark. It will be dark at 6:00 p.m. as we are on the equator, and then there is a danger of me not seeing any animals which might stray on to the road.'

Thankfully, the rest of the journey was uneventful, and they arrived at the hotel just before darkness fell. It was a large hotel just outside the town, with interesting views, a large garden and a big swimming pool at the back.

'Wow! This is cool!' Melody exclaimed when they were shown around. 'I'll get up and have a swim before breakfast every day.'

As they explored the hotel, the children were impressed but not overawed. It was cool, with tiled floors and air conditioning, but simply furnished. The three girls were sharing one very large bedroom, then their parents had a suite that included a sitting room, which they could all use, and Seb had a smaller room just opposite on the other side of the corridor.

The family quickly unpacked, showered and then went to the dining room for dinner. A large table had been assigned to them, near a window. It was very dark by now and the curtains had been pulled to keep out any insects that might be attracted by the lights.

Seb's Search

Candles that had a slight smell were burning on the table, and the family were told that these would keep mosquitoes at bay.

A young waiter brought their menus and spoke to Seb, obviously thinking he must be local.

'Agandi?' he greeted him, and Seb looked confused.

'Pardon,' he replied, 'I only speak English.'

'I'm sorry,' said the waiter. 'I apologise, but you look as if you are from the Ankole tribe; you have the features.'

Surprised, Seb explained that his ancestors came from Mbarara, but he was from England. The encounter was the beginning of a friendship between the two boys, which was to prove significant. The waiter's name was Emmanuel and he was the manager's son, working part-time in order to make enough money to help pay for his education.

The next couple of days the family spent around Mbarara, getting to know the town and enjoying the facilities at the hotel. Emmanuel spent as much time as he was able with Seb and was a mine of useful information.

'This isn't a town where people come to stay for holidays,' he told them. 'It's more of a stopping place as people travel from Kampala to the Rwenzori Mountains or to Rwanda or even to Burundi. We get lots of overnight visitors, but not as often families staying as you are. This is so good, because we can get to know each other and become friends.'

Emmanuel was studying at the boys' high school and hoping to get a place at university to study economics and tourism in order to return to the hotel and work there, helping his father.

Seb's Search

The children were amazed at how quickly it became very dark once the sun had set, and then they were able to see the most amazing display of stars! There was so little light pollution that the whole sky was filled with stars! Emmanuel knew many of the constellations and was happy to teach Seb and his sisters once he'd finished his work in the dining room.

On their third day, the family had a trip to one of the game parks in the area, Lake Mburo National Park. They set off very early, just before sunrise, in order to see as many animals as possible before it became too hot. The animals were more active early in the day. The park was well known for its herds of zebra. Elise had her sketchbook and pencils just in case she would have an opportunity to draw some. None of them knew what to expect but loved driving around the five lakes in the park, the largest of which is called Mburo. The paths were just dust tracks and there were thorn bushes and high grass, which made the zebra surprisingly difficult to spot.

'I had no idea that their stripes would be a sort of camouflage,' Rosa said. 'They kind of blend in with the tall grass and the sunlight.'

They had a park ranger to accompany them in their four by four, and he had binoculars and was trained to spot the animals in the bush. They saw several different kinds of antelope, and he told them their names. They were very shy creatures and scattered when they heard any noise.

By the side of the lake, the family were able to get out and look at the hippos and then trek with the ranger over a short distance. They saw herds of buffalo and Elise was able to sketch these as they grazed. The ranger explained they should beware of any lone buffalo, because they could be dangerous. In the park, they also saw herds of Ankole cattle, the very prized, although not wild, long-horned cattle for which the area is famous.

'These are the wealth of the people,' explained their ranger. 'They are given as dowries for brides and are more precious than actual money. Always be careful as you drive along the country roads, for to hit one would mean bad trouble.'

The ranger also pointed out many different species of birds to the Morris family. The most spectacular was the fish eagle, often seen on the top of the trees by the lakeside, but when they saw them in flight, they were amazed at how large the wingspan was—truly majestic birds. They were also able to see the little weaver birds and their hanging nests, and when they looked through the binoculars, it was awesome to see how beautifully crafted the nests were.

It was a truly amazing day, and they took so many photos to put on social media for their friends to see.

'I thought we would see lions and elephants and giraffes,' said Melody, a bit disappointed because she had hoped to see some big game.

'Be patient, young lady,' Dad replied. 'We plan to do another safari at the end of the holiday in an area where we should see some big game animals.'

– Chapter twelve –

Whereas most things they saw in Uganda were exciting and interesting, the family did find some sights hard to cope with.

'I hate seeing the little children on the side of the road carrying the yellow plastic cans to get the water,' Elise said to Emmanuel, when he was walking them into the town to shop. 'Even very tiny children seem to have to carry large loads on their heads. Some have such ragged clothes too.'

'When I was a child, I had to do many chores, for we were quite poor,' said Emmanuel. 'It's usual for children to get the water for the family before school. In the town, more houses now have mains water from taps, but not in the poorer areas. At least there are more wells these days and less people use water from the river—that causes many horrible diseases. Our tap water isn't safe to drink, especially for you mzungus. That's why you always need to buy bottled water or drink soda. Even my mother boils the tap water, then filters it, to be sure we all keep well.

'When my father got the job at the hotel and had promotions, things were easier for us, but there are still eight of us to send to school. That's why I work to help pay the fees as I go to a good school. If I get to university, then I should have a better chance of getting a good job and helping my younger brothers and sisters. I have many blessings compared with so many poor children in our country.'

Seb felt he was learning so much about his own blood people and their culture. Every night he wrote up a detailed diary. He had been challenged by George to learn all he could to share with his own children one day, should he ever have any.

One evening he was sitting by the pool with Emmanuel, looking at the stars as they often did, and he shared his story and the reason they had come to Mbarara with his new friend.

'Wow!' said Emmanuel. 'That's quite a story. So you know nothing about your birth mother?'

'Nothing at all,' replied Seb. 'We didn't come here to find her—that's impossible—but Mum and Dad thought I should visit the place she mentioned on the scrap of paper and learn about my heritage and culture. Mum and Dad are fantastic—I couldn't have had better parents or a better upbringing. I think God had chosen them for me, because for whatever reason, my birth mother couldn't take care of me and put me in the box and under the bush in the garden. When my triplet sisters were born, Mum made them all "birth boxes" like mine so that we are all the same. They have special little things in them too.'

'Well,' he added, getting up, 'I must say goodnight and get to bed because tomorrow we are going to the Queen Elizabeth National Park and will be away for a night in the lodge there.'

The boys went inside, little knowing that the pool attendant had overheard the whole story and a plan was forming in his mind!

Seb's Search

The next day, the family packed overnight bags, loaded the car and drove further west to the Queen Elizabeth National Park. The minute they entered the park gates, all of them felt the excitement rise as they kept their eyes open, looking at the countryside around them, hoping to see some wild animals.

It was a twenty-four kilometre drive from the perimeter gate to arrive at the main tourist centre, where they were to register and be shown their overnight accommodation. As they drove down the dirt track, they saw a herd of buffalo enjoying the mud of a large puddle and a family of warthogs scoot into the bushes. They looked so funny running with their tails up!

Just before they arrived at the tourist centre, Dad had to pull the car over to the side of the road as a small herd of elephants suddenly came out of the trees. The noise of their trumpeting was deafening, and the children found their hearts thumping in their chests as a very large elephant stepped out on to the road right next to where they had stopped, followed by several others and two babies! They were so close, and all the family took some amazing photos. It was a fantastic sight, but also a bit scary, because the elephants were so huge and noisy and had appeared so suddenly.

'Yay!' Rosa said, almost under her breath. 'I'll never, ever forget this. It's a memory for life.'

When the elephant family had crossed the road and passed to the other side, disappearing into the trees, Dad decided it was safe to start the engine again and drove to the registration point.

Seb's Search

'When you have found your room and eaten lunch, you are booked on a boat trip that starts at 3:00 p.m.,' they were told by the ranger. 'It lasts two hours and you will travel up the Kazinga Channel. You board the launch just below the Mweya Safari Lodge, where you will be staying. This track takes you there,' he said, pointing the way.

They found the lodge easily, and there were lots of other visitors staying there from many countries. The Morris family unpacked their bags and went to the restaurant where there was a huge buffet lunch with both Ugandan and European foods.

'There's so much to choose from,' Melody said. 'I don't know what to try first!'

'I do', replied Rosa. 'There's that lovely tilapia fish we tried before—and some chips too.'

Just before 3:00 p.m., they walked down to the launch. The boat was full of visitors and it left on time, which they had already discovered was an unusual event in Africa where everyone was much more laid-back about time than in England.

The Kazinga Channel is a strip of water that joins two lakes together, the large Lake Edward with the smaller Lake George. The launch slowly chugged up the channel, giving all the guests time to see the scenery. The ranger on-board told people where to look when he spotted anything unusual.

There were thousands of hippos! It was a bit unnerving to see so many of these huge beasts so near to the boat, but they must have been used to the launch doing several trips each day because they took no notice of it. The other animals which they

Seb's Search

saw in great numbers were pelicans. A herd of elephants was spotted in the distance, but they were not so easy to photograph as they were a long way away.

'I'm so glad I got good photos this morning,' remarked Seb. 'I can't wait to post them on Instagram for all my friends to see. This holiday is so cool—they'll all be so jealous!'

The boat trip was a great success, and they were back at the lodge in time to have cool drinks and then see a most amazing sunset before dinner.

'Very early to bed tonight, all of you,' Mum told them. 'We need to be ready to leave at 5:00 a.m. tomorrow. A park ranger will come with us in our car. Sleep well.'

It was hard to get to sleep after so much excitement. The girls were chatting for a while in their room about all their adventures.

'This is the most cool holiday we've ever had,' said Rosa, and Elise giggled.

'It's really the most *hot* one,' she said, 'but I know what you mean—it's amazing. We have Seb to thank for it. If we didn't have a Ugandan brother, we would never have come here.'

'I wonder what he feels about being in the country where his parents came from and yet not know anything about them. When you think about it, he could have lots of relatives living very near, but he wouldn't know them. I hope it doesn't make him feel any less one of us—he's a Morris still and our big brother,' commented Melody thoughtfully.

This made Elise think about Seb, and she prayed quietly that God would bless him and help him understand who he was, both Ugandan and British.

A very sleepy family emerged for the 5:00 a.m. start the next day. The ranger was waiting for them. He rode up front in the car alongside Dad and handed everyone a pair of binoculars to use.

'We are travelling to the northwestern boundary of the park,' he told them, 'near the foothills of the Rwenzori Mountains and the border with the Congo. Don't be scared because I carry a gun—that's routine as we used to have trouble with rebels from the Congo, but all is quiet now.'

Mum went a bit pale; she wasn't sure she wanted to know about rebel soldiers and guns. As they drove nearer the mountains, which used to be called by Ugandans 'the mountains of the moon' and were famous for their very lush growth of forest, they saw the sun rise. It was truly awesome—different from the sunset, but incredibly beautiful.

'Now we will drive into the savannah and hope to see some lions,' the ranger told them. 'I cannot promise you—we had so many wonderful animals killed when Idi Amin's regime ruled and the Tanzanian soldiers invaded to help fight against him. The war depleted our wildlife, but gradually through conservation the stock is slowly increasing.'

They drove on slowly, and suddenly the ranger told Dad to stop and everyone to be still and quiet. Then he pointed out a rock, and through their binoculars they saw a leopard stretched

Seb's Search

out. They held their breath in wonder as they saw not only the mother leopard but two babies suckling her.

They watched for a while, then Dad was told to drive again and the ranger directed him off the main track into thicker scrub.

'Stop,' he said quietly. 'Look over to the watering hole on your left.'

Once again with binoculars, they saw a pride of lions. There were three females and several cubs, drinking. They managed to get some photos, Mum's being the best as she had a telephoto lens.

'You are lucky people,' the ranger told them. 'Not many visitors see both leopard and lion.'

They were driving back to the main track when Dad noticed problems with the steering.

'Goodness, I think we have a puncture!' he told them. 'I'll have to change a wheel. Seb, can you help me?'

The three men got out of the car, and the ranger suggested that the girls and Mum stay put, even though they were hot. It didn't take too long to get the car jacked up and the punctured wheel off. It didn't take long for them to be noticed either! A troupe of interested chimpanzees soon appeared on the scene, jumping on the car and inspecting the windscreen wipers in great detail!

'Don't open the windows or the doors,' the ranger told them, 'and don't feed them. They look cute but are wild animals and can be destructive. Don't be scared. I'm going to fire a shot into the air to frighten them off before they do any real damage. Put your hands over your ears!'

The shot was loud and did scare everyone, not just the chimps. Very quickly the men put on the new wheel and they were all on their way again. They saw various kinds of antelope as they drove back, and the ranger also pointed out many birds, but it was hard to see them, even with binoculars.

It was lunchtime when they arrived back at the lodge. It had been a spectacular safari—a day they would never forget!

– Chapter thirteen –

The family were back in Mbarara that evening in time for dinner but were all very tired. Emmanuel was on duty, and Seb wanted to tell him about their adventures, so although the rest of the family went straight to bed, he and Emmanuel sat beside the pool in the garden for a while. Then Emmanuel said goodnight and left, but Seb remained sitting quietly for a few extra minutes, thanking God for the wonderful animals he had seen. Words came clearly into his mind, although they didn't make any sense: 'Don't be afraid, I am with you always.'

He knew God was speaking to him, and the words kept coming again and again. As he thought about the sentence, suddenly the lights around the pool went out, and he was in pitch darkness.

'I should go up to bed anyway,' he said to himself, reaching for his phone and switching on the torch function.

He heard a noise behind him and turned just as someone clamped a thick cloth over his nose and mouth. It smelt weird, a smell he couldn't place. He tried to scream and struggled to get free, almost falling into some bushes. His phone dropped out of his hand, and that was the last thing he remembered for some long time.

When he regained consciousness, Seb found that he was travelling, shut in a dark, small space, a gag over his mouth and his hands and his feet tied. It was bumpy, and he realised he must be in the boot of a car.

Vomit was coming up into his mouth and it was horrible, but because of the gag he couldn't get rid of it. His legs began to shake uncontrollably with terror. Whatever was happening to him? This was worse than the nightmares he used to have! If only he could move—if only he could get the cloth away from his mouth! Seb felt so helpless. Then the words came back into his mind: 'Don't be afraid, I am with you always.'

'Oh Jesus, help me,' he prayed in his mind, then drifted back into unconsciousness.

He woke to find the boot of the car being opened, and he was pulled out by two men, one of whom he recognised by his voice, although he didn't understand the language. He was sure it was the pool attendant from the hotel.

Seb was bundled into a little mud hut, and the ropes on his legs and arms were cut and the gag taken from his mouth. Stunned, he wanted to shout and scream, but he still felt woozy and words wouldn't come out. The men quickly left, and he heard the car drive away.

It was very dark inside the hut, the windows had shutters that seemed to be bolted from the outside, and the door was padlocked. The darkness was terrifying, and the smell in the hut was horrible. Seb was still sweating and shaking, but this was no nightmare from which he would wake up, put on the light and feel safe again. This was real. He'd been kidnapped—but why?

Seb's Search

His head began to thump, and Seb lay down on the earthen floor. He curled into a ball, trying not to cry, and finally fell asleep again.

When he woke, he could see a little daylight coming under the door and shafts of light where the shutters didn't quite fit. He strained his ears and could hear people's voices, then steps approaching the hut. His body tensed all over. What would happen next?

He heard the bolt being moved and almost had to shield his eyes as the daylight flooded in.

A small boy came in, with a tin mug and plate.

'Good morning. My name is Kaba. What is your name?' he said in English, just as if it were a lesson or they had been introduced somewhere. It was so unexpected that Seb almost burst out laughing.

'Agandi,' he replied, greeting the child in Runyankole. 'My name is Seb. How are you?'

'I am fine, thank you,' the child replied. 'I have food.' He handed the plate and mug to Seb.

'Ugali,' the boy said, pointing to the plate, 'and chai,' pointing to the mug.

'Thank you, Kaba,' Seb replied politely. It was such a weird charade, he didn't know what to say but had the overwhelming need to laugh.

Seb knew what chai was—a sweet, milky tea with spices, which they had already tried in Uganda. At least he could drink it because he knew that the water and milk were boiled together when it was made so germs would be killed. This thought made him worry—he didn't have his antimalarial tablets with him, and he had lots of mosquito bites already after his night in the hut.

He sipped the tea, then looked at the ugali. It looked horrible—a mass of greyish goo. He looked up at Kaba.

'How do I eat?' he asked.

The boy giggled, then came and sat on the floor by Seb. He pulled a little piece away from the huge grey lump, rolled it into a ball and popped it into his mouth. Although it looked so unappetizing, Seb was hungry and he knew he needed to eat, so he copied the boy. He thought he would never swallow the stuff but managed somehow to get it down. He tried to smile and had another swig of the chai.

Kaba smiled too and said, 'Good.'

Seb continued to eat as much as he could manage of the cold, grey glue-like meal and washed it down with the tea.

He needed the loo. Now that was a dilemma. When they had stayed in Lubowa, the children there had taught him the word 'afuse', but that had been in their language. By now, however, Seb was pretty desperate, so he spoke the word urgently.

Kaba smiled again and said, 'Yes—come,' and led Seb outside to an outhouse—a disgusting latrine. Seb held his nose but went in and did what he needed to.

Then he had a look around him. It didn't occur to him that he could run away. He was obviously somewhere in the country. Besides the small hut where he had been imprisoned the night before, there was another mud house, larger with a tin roof.

Seb's Search

Behind the house he was able to see a shack, which he thought was probably the kitchen, and a woman with a baby tied on her back was tending a large cooking pot. Around the house were a few bushes, and some clothes were on these. Seb guessed they must be washing put out to dry.

Kaba smiled and pointed to the woman. 'Mama,' he said. 'Now back to room. I go to school.' He led Seb back to the hut, opened the windows, removed the dish and mug and locked the door. It was horrible being locked in once again, but at least now there was some light.

Seb saw a cloth on the floor and a blanket. Maybe that was supposed to be his bed. He felt so miserable inside. Whatever must his parents be thinking? They would be so worried—and his sisters too. Why had he been kidnapped? Did someone think he belonged in Uganda and should stay here? The thought horrified him.

Then he thought about his birth mother. Had she returned to Uganda, and did she live in these sorts of conditions? What about the young boy Kaba? What chances in life would he have? He remembered the words that had come into his mind just before he had been kidnapped. They had seemed so strange then, but now they were comforting. He prayed and asked Jesus to help him, to keep him safe and get him back to his family.

– Chapter fourteen –

Emmanuel had gone to his room in the apartment where his family lived in the hotel and was getting ready for bed when he noticed the lights around the pool had gone out. He thought it was a bit odd, since they were on a timer and scheduled to be switched off at midnight.

'Maybe something has fused,' he thought. 'I must remember to tell Dad before I go to school tomorrow.'

He also heard some noises but thought nothing of it; it was probably only a cat or a dog in the garden.

The next morning, Emmanuel left for school before the guests woke up for breakfast, speaking to his father first about the pool lights.

Seb's parents were at the breakfast table and had placed their orders, and then the girls appeared. After a while, Dad decided he should go and see if Seb was awake. He had some plans for the day and had told them all he wanted to leave around eleven. It was unlike Seb to be late for food!

Dad knocked on the door, and when he heard no answer, he opened it. There was no sign of his son in the room or in the en suite. The bed was made up, and everything looked as if he hadn't been there all night.

Seb's Search

A cold shudder of fear went through Mr Morris. Something must be up—something awful must have happened. He knew his son would never have gone off on his own without asking first.

He ran down the stairs two at a time to the dining room. He looked white with shock.

'Seb's not in his room. I don't think he's been there all night because it's just as room service would have left it after cleaning. They don't start cleaning until midday, so it hasn't just been done. Have you girls seen or heard him today?'

'No,' they all replied. 'Last thing was after dinner. He went for a quick chat with Emmanuel as usual and we went straight to bed.'

'Stay here,' Dad told the girls. 'Mum and I must go and talk to the manager.'

They went straight to the manager's office and told him what had happened. The manager was very distressed and called Emmanuel's school to ask for his son to come home at once. Then he called the ground staff and asked them to search all the hotel gardens, in case Seb had fallen outside, and the housekeeping staff to search everywhere in the hotel.

Emmanuel came running home from school, very upset. He told them all he knew, including the pool lights going out and the noises he'd heard but thought they were probably from animals.

'I think we should call the police,' Emmanuel's father decided. 'As soon as they arrive, I'll call your room. I suggest your family stay in your sitting room until we have some news. I will arrange coffee to be sent there for you. Emmanuel will do that,

Seb's Search

won't you? Meanwhile I must just check the pool lights. I don't understand why they went off early.'

The family went up to their room as requested, and the coffee arrived. Emmanuel was clearly as confused and upset as they were.

'Stay and have coffee with us,' invited Mrs Morris, as she poured it out. Not that anyone needed coffee so soon after breakfast, but it gave them something to do.

'I'm going to text Jake and the pastor,' said Elise. 'I know they will pray for us all and for Seb to be found quickly.'

'Good idea, and I'll phone Naomi and George. They might know what to do,' Mum said. 'I'll just go to the bedroom for a few minutes and phone from there.'

She had been gone for only a few seconds when she came back in crying.

'Mum, what is it?' asked Rosa.

Her mum was distraught and had a piece of paper in her hand.

'This note has been pushed under our door—Seb's been kidnapped and this is a ransom note,' she sobbed, handing the piece of paper to her husband.

'Emmanuel, can you go and tell your father and ask him to come up?' Mr Morris requested. 'Meanwhile, I will phone George. We need help quickly.'

George was at work in Kampala, but fortunately not with a client, so he was able to talk at length to Seb's father. The demand the kidnapper was making was a large sum of Ugandan

Seb's Search

shillings, and George advised them not to meet the demand but to involve the police. He would fly up to the small airstrip at Mbarara as soon as possible to be with them. Flying would be quicker than driving.

It wasn't long before the police arrived. The inspector came to talk to the family, while some of his officers scoured the grounds for clues and others set up an incident room in the hotel and began to interview the staff one by one. The first piece of good news came when one of the police officers found Seb's phone in the bushes. Some leaves were also torn from the bush and lying on the ground, so they surmised that that was where the kidnapping had taken place. Since the pool's lights were in good order, they deduced that someone connected with the kidnapping had deliberately switched them off, but who knew how to do that?

Emmanuel was terrified to find that he was the number-one suspect. He knew Seb's story, and whoever wrote the note had known that Seb was abandoned at birth and then adopted. He had been the last person to see Seb that night and had reported the lights being off to his father.

The inspector wanted to take him to the prison at once, but his father and the Morris family intervened, and it was agreed he should stay locked in his bedroom for the time being, guarded by a policeman.

'We know what good friends you and Seb are,' Melody told the frightened boy. 'We know you would not have done such a thing. How could you have managed it anyway? He's as big as you are and very strong!'

Fingerprints were taken from the phone, but they didn't match any from the staff. The pool light switches did have fingerprints on them and they were from the pool attendant, so he was interviewed by the inspector and detained as the number-two suspect. He appeared very nervous and anxious when questioned by the police, but there was no real evidence of him being the kidnapper. He was not happy when he was told that he must remain on the premises until further notice and told the police he needed to get home to his family.

It was a relief when George arrived. He was a well known and highly respected lawyer in Kampala and knew exactly how to advise the family. Naomi had flown up with him, and that was a comfort to Seb's mum and the girls. The day seemed endless, and Rosa, Melody and Elise tried to play games to distract themselves, but it didn't work. They were all too worried about Seb and his safety.

The day seemed endless to Seb too, with nothing to do and no one to talk to. In the middle of the afternoon, Kaba came back from school and went to see that the prisoner was alright.

'I need a drink, please,' Seb begged, for his mouth was parched and dry. He was afraid of becoming dehydrated. The children had been told they needed to drink at least six bottles of water every day while staying in Uganda to avoid becoming dehydrated.

Seb's Search

Kaba came back with a cup of very dirty-looking water, and Seb tried to explain that he needed a bottle from a shop. He fished around in his pocket for some shillings and handed it to Kaba.

'Please,' he said, 'water from a duka.' Duka was the word for a small shop; Emmanuel had taught him that.

The boy nodded and trotted away, forgetting to lock the door. Seb slipped out to the latrine, then looked around, noting the path which Kaba had taken. He still had his watch, so he timed how long it took the boy to get to the nearest little shop and back, because that would give him some idea of where the nearest village might be. He just hoped and prayed that the boy, who seemed friendly, would in fact buy water and not run off with his money.

It was too hot to stay outside for long, so he sat in the doorway and eventually saw Kaba coming up the track carrying two large bottles of water and a paper bag. The bottles were sealed, much to Seb's relief, and so were good to drink from. He wanted to swig the whole lot down at once, but then common sense told him to drink it little by little and make it last.

Kaba held out the bag in which were little sweet bananas. 'I buy for you to eat,' he told Seb.

'Oh, thank you,' said Seb in delight, peeling one and trying to eat it slowly. There were six in the bag, so Seb held one out to Kaba, who beamed with happiness as he ate it.

From the pocket of his khaki shorts, the boy produced a few small coins, obviously change from the shopping, and handed them back to Seb, who shook his head.

'No, you can keep it.'

Once again, the boy's face creased into a very big smile, and he said, 'Thank you.'

If only Kaba knew a little more English, I could find out where I am and what this is all about, thought Seb. At least we are friends now and trust each other.

– Chapter fifteen –

Later in the evening, when it was dark once again and Seb was locked up in the hut, Kaba came to visit him. He carried more food—this time a plate of yellow mush, covered with a grey-coloured sauce, and a mug of chai. It was so dark, even with the door open, so Kaba ran back to the house and returned with a Tilley paraffin lamp. Seb had never before seen anything like it, but he was glad of the soft glow of light that it gave.

'Matoke,' said Kaba, pointing to the yellow food. 'Very good.'

He showed Seb how to scoop up a handful with his fingers, dip it into the sauce, which tasted of peanuts, and put it into his mouth. It tasted a bit strange, but much better than the ugali Seb'd eaten for breakfast.

In the background he heard a woman shouting.

'Mama needs me,' said Kaba. 'She's *kali* (angry) today. Papa not home with money from your papa. When he get money, you go to your papa. Good evening, Mr Seb,' Kabi said solemnly, as he took away the empty plate, mug and light.

He locked the door, and once again Seb was left in the darkness, though this time he wasn't so afraid. He felt that Kaba was a friend, and he understood that once a ransom had been paid, he would be given back to his family. All the kidnapper wanted was money.

Seb's Search

There was a sense of peace, even in the darkness, and Seb knew that just as he had promised, Jesus was with him, and he sang some songs that he'd learnt at the chapel youth group, then talked to Jesus before he lay down to sleep.

In the middle of the night, Seb was woken by a weird feeling and a noise he couldn't place.

He sat up and rubbed his eyes. No, he wasn't dreaming. He felt as if he were in London travelling on the underground train, rattling along. That was what the sound reminded him of—a deep, rumbling noise. He felt very disturbed and then felt sure the ground underneath him was moving. Then the awful thought came into his mind—could it be an earthquake? That was the sort of disaster you saw on television, but this was real.

Panic started to rise inside him. He was locked inside this hut—would he survive? He started to scream, then in his head once again he heard the words: 'Do not be afraid, I am with you always.'

Seb screamed back to God. 'Then get me out of here now, before I die!'

He heard the bolt being drawn back on the door and a very scared little Kaba looking at him.

'Come out,' he yelled and then began speaking rapidly in his own tongue.

In seconds, Seb joined him outside. His first thought was that now he could run away—get away from this nightmare—but Kaba was holding his hand and pointing over to the house. Part of it had fallen down.

Seb's Search

'Mama, Mama,' the boy screamed. Seb knew he couldn't run away and leave the lad. He ran with him to the house. It was a horrible sensation, the earth rumbling and moving beneath you. At the house he saw the problem at once. Kaba's mother was trapped by a large wooden pole that had fallen on her leg. Near her on the floor was the baby, who was crying.

Gently, Seb picked up the baby and gave her to Kaba, telling him to lay her on the ground far from the house and not near a building or a tree, then to come back and help him. How much the lad understood he had no idea, but he took the baby away and came back within a few minutes.

Seb looked at the pole. It was holding up part of the roof, but he reckoned if they could ease it gently to one side, they might be able to release the woman's leg and drag her outside. It was the only chance, and although it meant risking their lives, he prayed that they would be alright.

With sign language and a few simple words, he tried to explain, and as he lifted the pole very slowly—and it was heavy— Kaba pulled his mother's leg free. She screamed in pain and then fainted.

Seb then somehow managed to lift the woman by her shoulders, and with Kaba holding the injured leg, they dragged her outside and as far away from the building as they could manage. It was so hard because of the darkness, but there was a full moon, which helped a lot. Kaba seemed much more used to seeing in the dark that Seb was, and he quickly ran to retrieve his baby sister and place her in his mama's arms. The mother was awake again, but in a lot of pain.

Seb tried to remember the first aid he had been taught in primary school. He needed to splint the leg to hold the bones together—but what could he use? He knew it would be risky to go into the house, but he thought about what he'd seen in the kitchen area—when the woman had been cooking, she had used a huge wooden spoon.

He tried to tell Kaba what he wanted and eventually the lad seemed to understand his acting and went running to get the spoon. He came back with two and handed them to Seb, who had remembered the cloth in the hut where he was lying and ran to get it, tore it into some strips and used the strips to bandage the broken leg to the spoons. It wasn't ideal, and the woman was screaming while he did it, but he knew it was better than nothing.

Now he needed to get help. After a few minutes' thought, Seb decided that it would be best to send Kaba for help as he knew the path to the shop. He hated to send the small boy on such a difficult journey in the dark. He knew that trees might have fallen down or holes opened up in the earth, but since the rumbling had stopped he hoped that it had been either a small earthquake or that they were not too near the epicentre.

'Kaba,' he said, 'go to the duka and get help. I'll look after Mama and baby.' Seb wished so much he had his phone—he could have got help quickly. He gave the boy a hug and sat down by his mother, whom he had covered with the blanket from the

Seb's Search

hut where he had been imprisoned. He was cold, and now that the worst of the crisis had passed, was shivering from shock.

Kaba's mother had stopped screaming and was feeding her baby. She seemed to accept Seb's presence. As he sat there in the cold, it made him wonder about his birth mother and what a hard life it was for poor people in rural Uganda. Perhaps she had wanted a better life for him and that was why she gave him away. He wondered how she came to be in London and if she ever returned to Mbarara.

It seemed a very long wait, but eventually Seb saw some lights coming up the path. Kaba was back with two adults.

'Thank you, Jesus,' Seb said out loud. He was so relieved.

- Chapter Sixteen -

The Morris family had spent a sleepless night longing for good news about Seb. George and Naomi had been pillars of strength for them, advising and helping and praying with them.

George had gone with Dad and an undercover policeman to take a package to the place where the ransom note had told them to be. They had waited and waited, but no one had appeared. That made the policeman think that perhaps one of the suspects who were locked in rooms at the hotel might be the kidnapper.

The family had prayed together for Seb's safety and welfare. Mum was most concerned that he might develop dysentery from infected water or food and that he had no antimalarial drugs with him, but Naomi reassured her that these things could be quickly dealt with once he was found.

Each of the suspects had a policeman guarding them in their room. Emmanuel had been very upset and kept asking if Seb had been found. He tried to do some school homework to pass the time, but it was difficult to concentrate. He put the TV on every now and then, but still the time dragged by. Sometimes the policeman talked to him, and his father was allowed to be with him at times. As the day wore on, it seemed to the policeman less and less likely that Emmanuel had anything to do with the disappearance of Seb.

Seb's Search

The pool attendant, however, became very agitated as they day wore on and would not answer any of the policeman's questions. He kept asking for a lawyer, but when George was brought in to talk to him, he looked very scared and refused to talk to him too. At one point in the day, his car keys had been taken and his car was searched and forensic samples taken. These had been sent to Kampala to the laboratory. The police hoped to get some results quickly, but it was a five-hour drive to take things to the capital, let alone be processed and send back results.

The policeman guarding the pool attendant had the television on most of the time. The local news told of the kidnapping, and he watched the prisoner very carefully to see his reaction. The next morning, when he put the TV on, he had a reaction which was quite unexpected. The main news item was an earthquake that had occurred during the night in the town of Fort Portal and the surrounding area. The pool attendant began to shake as he saw the pictures of the devastation both in the town and in surrounding villages.

'I need to go home. My wife and children are at my village house—' the attendant hesitated, '—and a visitor. I must know they are not hurt.'

'And who is this visitor?' questioned the policeman, for he sensed that his prisoner knew more than he was saying. 'If it is the lost child, then it will be all the worse for you if he is hurt or killed in the earthquake—you could be charged with murder!'

Seb's Search

At this, the pool attendant broke down. 'Yes, it is him. The rich Ugandan boy. I heard his story when he told his friend. I knew I could make some money for my own son to go to a good school and have a better life too. Now I do not know if either of them is alive, or my wife or my baby daughter.'

Even the hardened police officer was moved when he heard this and saw the prisoner's distress. It was for real, not faked. He picked up his phone, called the inspector, then the hotel manager, and asked them to come as quickly as they were able and to bring Seb's father too.

The hotel manager arrived first and immediately was told that his son was in the clear and could be released and that the officer guarding him could come to the meeting. Then the manager collected Mr Morris, reassuring him that it wasn't bad news.

'I'll be back as soon as I can and tell you what's happening,' he told his wife and daughters, as he went to the room where the prisoner was being held.

As soon as the inspector was with them, the pool attendant confessed his whole story and his fears for his family and Seb, with great remorse.

'Let's get out there and find them. If they have been affected by the earthquake, they may need urgent help,' the inspector responded. 'You'll be transferred to the town jail and formally charged,' he informed the sobbing prisoner. 'We will tell you if your family are safe when we find them.'

George told Seb's father that he would go with him and the police inspector, while Naomi would stay with the rest of the

Seb's Search

family. In a very short while, they were on their way to the Fort Portal area, with detailed instructions about the precise location of where the house was situated. The local police were to meet them there.

'Let's go into the garden,' suggested Rosa. 'We need to do something while we wait.'

'There's a volleyball net out there,' Melody informed them. 'Let me find out where the balls are kept. I really need some exercise to take my mind off all the worries.'

Emmanuel was still in the hotel and found the balls for the girls.

'Can I play too?' he asked. 'I can't stop thinking about Seb either and don't want to go back to school today.'

With Mum and Naomi joining them, they played in rotation and all felt better for some vigorous exercise, even managing to joke and laugh a bit, but everyone was listening intently for a phone to ring.

Meanwhile, the men were travelling north at breakneck speed in a police minibus with a siren attached. It wasn't so bad on the tarmac roads, but when they turned off onto mud roads, the red dust covered them, coming in through cracks even though the windows were closed.

As they approached Kibale Forest National Park, the wardens warned them that some tracks were closed due to the earthquake and fallen trees. Then they continued more slowly until they arrived to the small village where Kaba had bought the water. The pool attendant had told them it was the nearest village to his house, so they asked around for news.

George was a great help as many village people were afraid to talk to the police, so he asked them questions clearly and gently. He could see some houses had been badly damaged and that the people were shaken by the events of the previous night. He was led to the duka and learnt the story of the family who had needed help in the night. The shopkeeper told them that the boys and the baby had been taken to a hospital near Kasese, along with the mother who had a broken leg. They were informed that the children were unharmed, and the van turned around to drive a little way southwest to the hospital.

The news was relayed through the police shortwave radio to the family at the hotel that they were now headed for Kasese and it seemed that only the mother was injured. The relief that everyone felt was so great. The girls gave a great cheer, and their mum was almost in tears with sheer joy.

The police van's brakes screeched as the vehicle pulled into the hospital forecourt, and the men jumped out. People standing around the entrance scattered, seeing the policemen rush in followed first by someone who looked important and then a mzungu guy. They wondered what was happening—things like that didn't often happen in their small town. Little children fled behind their mother's skirts and then peeked out at times to see the action. Inside, hospital staff stopped what they were doing and offered help.

Seb's Search

Very soon they were taken to a ward where a woman was lying on a bed, cuddling a baby, and Seb and Kaba sat on the floor, the older boy trying to comfort the younger one. They jumped up when the men came in, Seb rushing into his dad's arms and almost crying with relief but trying not to do so in front of little Kaba. Everyone began to talk at once.

'This won't do,' said the nursing sister. 'I have sick patients here. Please talk quietly or go outside.'

'I'll stay here to talk to the patient,' said the inspector. 'You men take the boys outside and talk to them.'

A veranda ran around the outside of the single-story hospital building. George and Seb's father took the boys to sit on a bench and listened while they told their stories. Seb first of all told his dad all that had happened to him, from the time he was kidnapped until he reached the hospital.

'I wanted to get a phone message to you, but the main mast was destroyed by the earthquake, we were told, so no messages could be sent. I had also given the rest of my money to help pay for treatment for Kaba's mum.'

Meanwhile, George knew enough Runyankole to speak to Kaba in his own language and find out what had happened. Kaba told George how brave Seb had been and that without his help his mother may not have survived. He cried a little, for he was only eight years old, as he said he didn't know where his father was since he hadn't arrived home as expected the previous day. He understood that his father had done a bad thing to steal the boy and lock him up, but he didn't know why he had done so.

After the policeman had satisfied himself that the prisoner's wife had not been involved in the kidnapping but had only been told by her husband to feed Seb and keep him locked up until he returned, he came to the veranda and discussed the situation with the other men.

'I think we should take Seb back to Mbarara now and leave the little boy to look after his mother and the baby. The mother needs an operation. I have spoken to the nurse and made sure that they will all get food, but it will be necessary to check in a few days' time that all is well and see if the house can be repaired.'

George, knowing how things worked in a Ugandan hospital, spoke to the administrator, leaving money to cover any urgent needs and promising Kaba that everything would be taken care of.

'Look, Dad, look!' said Seb in excitement as they were leaving the hospital. 'There's a plaque here—please take a photo for me on your phone. It says that Sir Cliff Richard came here!'

'Goodness me,' said his dad in amazement. 'So it does—a long time ago now. Mum will be interested—she's always been one of his biggest fans!'

– Chapter seventeen –

In the police van driving back to Mbarara, Seb slept. So much had happened, and he was exhausted by lack of sleep. Even though he wanted to tell everything to his dad in detail, his eyes just wouldn't keep open. Dad gently woke him up as they approached the town.

'Everyone's waiting for you, son. You'd better wake up!'

Seb stretched and rubbed his eyes, blinking at the strong sunlight. How he'd needed that sleep! Now his adventure almost seemed like a dream, and he felt none the worse for it.

It seemed as if all the hotel staff as well as his family were waiting at the door as they arrived home. They clapped and cheered, and he was most embarrassed by all the fuss. The best thing ever was being able to have a long, warm shower and dress in clean clothes again. An amazing meal had been prepared by the hotel staff for the family, friends, Emmanuel and the policemen who had helped find Seb.

'This tastes *so* good,' Seb said, tucking into the delicious food. 'That ugali stuff I had to eat was *disgusting*!'

The Ugandans around him laughed.

'It's fine if it's been well made and is served with other nice food, but cold, lumpy ugali on its own does leave something to be desired,' agreed Naomi.

Seb's Search

After they had eaten, the youngsters went to the garden and chatted together. The girls wanted to hear all about Seb's adventures. He was very upset when he heard that Emmanuel had been held as a suspect and locked in his room until the case was solved. The more Seb heard about Kaba's father and the reason he had kidnapped him, the sadder he felt. All the anger he had experienced while it was happening to him disappeared. He just felt terribly sad that the family were so poor and now had lost their home as well as Kaba's mother being injured and his dad being in prison.

The next morning George and Naomi flew back to Kampala.

There were not many days left of the family holiday, but Dad had decided to give the children a couple of extra treats as they'd experienced so much trauma and anxiety over the past few days. He arranged a trip back to Kasese and then on to visit the Rwenzori Mountains. He'd also decided to leave Mbarara a little earlier than originally planned and stop a night near Masaka on their way back to Kampala to visit Lake Nabugabo.

'Please, Dad, would it be possible for Emmanuel to join us on the trip to the Rwenzori Mountains?' Seb asked. 'He would so love that!'

'I plan to take you on Saturday, so if he's free, that's a great idea,' answered Dad. 'We'll just be doing a short trek. Mountain climbing is out of our league—even Melody's.'

Then Seb had a thought. 'Since we're going via Kasese, please could we call at the hospital and make sure Kaba and his mum are OK, Dad? I do wish his father could be given bail or

Seb's Search

something like that. I'm not hurt and although he did wrong, his family are going to suffer so much. Do you think there's anything we can do to get him released?'

'I don't know, son, but I'll have a word with Emmanuel's father and see if he thinks anything might be possible, and then we can go and see the police inspector.'

It was highly unusual in their culture, but Emmanuel's father was willing to have the pool attendant keep his job should he be allowed out on bail, because he was very good at his job and up until the kidnapping had never caused any trouble.

Seb, his dad and Emmanuel's father visited the police station and discussed the situation with the inspector, who noted on his report that the Morris family didn't want to press charges. The inspector was most surprised by the request and couldn't promise anything, but he did promise to email Mr Morris when the court hearing had taken place and judgement had been passed. Dad left money to pay the bail charges so that Kaba's father could be released into the hotel manager's care and police supervision until the trial took place.

'Thank you all so much. I hope the judge will be lenient when the trial happens,' Seb said with tears in his eyes, for he was really concerned about the family.

On Saturday morning, the Morris family and Emmanuel were up just before dawn. They had been advised about the gear they would need for a small trek on the lower mountain slopes. Even their food was wrapped in waterproof bags—everywhere was wet in the tropical forest on the lower slopes!

A bit sleepy but very excited, they drove to the town of Kasese, stopping at the Margherita Hotel, which was a few miles out of the town on a road which used to lead to some copper mines many years ago. The hotel was a spectacular building, with a magnificent view of the mountains.

By now everyone was fully awake and very hungry. They sat on the terrace and ate a huge breakfast, looking out at Mount Stanley, of which the highest peak was called Margherita, which was why the hotel was so named. It was fabulous. They were told that Mount Stanley had snow on its peaks all year and there were glaciers.

'There are legends about the mountains,' Emmanuel informed them. 'Everything which grows or lives in the mountains is reputed to be huge, larger than life. People say there are giants living there and fruits on the trees so heavy that they can't be carried in a person's hand. I'm sure the tales are exaggerated, because they are folk legends, but the mountains are very big, with snow on the top of most, and years ago many people came from Europe to climb them. Then there was the rule of Idi Amin followed by the war to depose him, and people stopped coming. That's why Kasese is no longer a big town, but now the tourists are slowly starting to come again.'

'Did I see an old railway line when we drove through?' asked Rosa. 'I didn't know you had trains here.'

'My grandfather tells of the time when he was young, when there was a train which went from Kasese to Kampala and from there you could travel on to Kenya and the Indian Ocean. There

Seb's Search

used to be copper mines at Kilembe, and that's why the train came out here. This was once an important town, and mzungu people came to stay in this hotel. I have never seen a train, but he told me all about them.'

After breakfast they went in the car to the entrance of Rwenzori Mountains National Park. A ranger came with them on the trek and a porter to help with even the comparatively small amount of gear they needed. They hired boots and sticks and set off.

It was amazing going through the forest track—the damp, misty smell, the huge trees and bushes dripping with drops of water which made them sparkle like jewels. Elise wished she could just stop and draw but had to be content with taking lots of photos. They could hear insects and birds, but it was hard to see them because the tree canopy and vegetation was so thick. Even the boys and Melody, who were the fittest of the group, found that they struggled a bit with getting their breath.

There were several different species of monkeys who scuttled across the paths. From time to time as they walked higher in the foothills, the mist cleared, revealing amazing views of the mountains.

They ate their lunch in a small but well-equipped mountain hut. Here they could make a hot drink, for it was surprisingly cold. The ranger and the porter told them that it was good they had visited in August, as it wasn't as wet and cold as at other times of the year.

Seb's Search

After a rest it was time to trek back to the entrance of the park. They had been told that serious climbers took a week to reach the top of Mount Stanley or one of the other mountains.

'It makes me want to take up mountaineering and come back here one day,' remarked Melody.

'Then I'll come with you and stay on the lower slopes and do botanical painting,' quipped Elise.

'And I'll come to visit Emmanuel,' was Seb's reply.

'I won't be left behind—triplets stay together!' was Rosa's comment, and they all laughed.

Once again, they stopped at the hotel before they went to visit the hospital. Seb not only wanted to see Kaba's family but he also wanted to show his family the plaque and photos of Sir Cliff Richard who had visited Kagando Hospital with a charity called Tearfund years ago.

When they went to the ward, it was a relief to find that Kaba's mother was recovering well after an operation to pin and plate her leg. Kaba was very excited to see Seb again and to meet Emmanuel and Seb's sisters.

Mrs Morris, being a nurse herself, was very interested in the hospital and was shown around by one of the nursing sisters. There was a distinct smell about it, very different from the disinfectant smell that many UK hospitals have. She could see how hard the nurses were working in very difficult circumstances. At the back of the hospital was an area where relatives slept and cooked food for the patients.

'What about Keba and his family?' she asked the sister.

Seb's Search

'The bush telegraph works well, and once his mother's relatives heard the house was destroyed and she was injured, they came to take care of her. They will take her and the children into their home for as long as necessary. They know the father is in some trouble, but in Uganda, the family will always care for each other. That is our way.'

'And a very good way too,' answered Seb's mother. 'I find it very sad in England when some old people have no one to care for them because all the families live so far away.'

The Morris family were able to leave some more money for the family's urgent needs before saying goodbye and driving back to Mbarara. It was dark by the time they reached the hotel and they were all very tired, but it had been a great day.

'I'm going to write it up in my diary at once,' declared Rosa. 'I don't want to forget a minute of the day.'

- Chapter eighteen -

It was quite hard to pack up and say goodbye to all their new friends at the hotel in Mbarara, but especially to Emmanuel. At least they could keep in touch by phone and the internet.

It helped a little to leave in that they were having one more adventurous stop on their way back to Kampala. Near Masaka, the town halfway on their journey to the capital, at a place called Lake Nabugabo, was a small lakeside resort where they would spend their next night. The lake was small, but the waters were clear and free from the disease of bilharzia, so it was safe for swimming. The hotel had little round houses for families, and these had lounges as well as bedrooms and bathroom and meals available at a central restaurant. It was such a pleasant, relaxing way to end the holiday and gave the family time to just have fun together, splashing around in the lake.

Sitting outside the 'banda' as the little house was called, watching the sun go down and hearing the noises of the birds and insects, the family were discussing the highlights of the holiday.

Elise was looking through her sketchbook, each page reminding her of the places they had visited and the animals and plants they had seen.

Seb's Search

'I'm looking forward to getting home again now,' she said. 'I want to paint some proper pictures from the sketches before I forget the vivid colours.'

'I'll never forget this holiday either,' commented Rosa. 'It's helped me think about my future, and I know I want to help people, maybe as a nurse or a social worker. I want to help sick and poor people.'

Melody was thoughtful for a few minutes before sharing her thoughts. 'I've loved this trip. It's helped me to realise how privileged we are in England. We have great school facilities, we never go hungry and we all probably will be able to get good jobs. I thought that maybe I could do some sporting events and get sponsored. It would be really cool to be able to raise some money for kids like Kaba so that they could do well in school.'

The girls continued to chat with Mum about all they had enjoyed on the holiday, but Dad suggested that he and Seb wander by the lake together.

'I'm so sorry, Seb,' his father told him. 'I truly wanted this to be a wonderful experience for you. I never dreamt anything bad would happen to you. I feel so guilty too, because it's my job to take care of you all and I failed you.'

'Please, Dad,' responded Seb, 'just put that out of your mind. This holiday has been amazing—all of it. I understand much more who I am and that my birth mother maybe was as poor as Kaba's mother. I am so grateful she left me under your bush—she gave me the gift of you and Mum, and you are the best parents in the world.

'When I was kidnapped, I was terrified, but in my head I clearly heard Jesus telling me he was with me and all would be ok. In that dark hut, that first night, I had time to think of lots of things, but it was ok. When the earthquake happened, I wanted to run away and try to get back to you, but then I knew I couldn't leave an eight-year-old who had been kind to me to cope with his injured mother and baby sister. I knew I wanted to do what Jesus would have done in the circumstances—stayed to help. That time as a captive taught me so much that I'm sort of glad in one way that it happened, except for the worry for you all.

'Dad, there is something I want to do when we get home. Please can I ask the pastor at church to baptise me? I know that I want to always follow Jesus. Even in that awful hut, he didn't leave me, and I knew everything would be alright.'

'Seb, I have no objection at all, and I suspect it will make your Grandma and Auntie Apple *very* pleased. Mum and I have also decided that we need to sign up to the course they have at the chapel to find out more about the Christian faith. We need God in our lives and in our family life.'

After this rather serious talk, they raced each other back to the banda to get ready to go for supper. Wonderful food aromas were wafting down from the restaurant, where a fresh fish barbeque was on the menu. They were able to eat outside on the veranda, with candles burning to keep away the mosquitoes and throwing a soft light into the African night.

'We need to leave early tomorrow to reach Kampala by lunchtime,' Dad told them all. 'I have to return the car, and

Seb's Search

George and Naomi are then taking us back to Lubowa for a few hours before we go to the airport, so early night for us all!'

Everything went according to plan the following day. The family were sorry to say goodbye to George and Naomi, but they promised to keep in touch by email. Rosa was taking some gifts back to Sophie from her cousin, and they had all bought little souvenirs for their friends as well as for themselves to remember the most fantastic holiday any of them had ever experienced.

It was good to get back to Gorsley. One of their aunties had looked after the chickens and Grandma had been shopping, filling the fridge with fresh food. She'd also baked them a casserole for their tea.

'Come on, Seb, you and I have one other job to do,' Dad told his son the next morning.

They jumped into the car and drove around to the dog rescue centre.

'Rix!' shouted Seb in delight, for the dog was waiting for them in the office. He jumped up and licked Seb's hands and face in delight.

'You belong to us now, Rix, forever and ever,' Seb told him. 'You're like me, adopted into the most fantastic family ever! We'll have such fun together—you came out of a basket and I came out of a box!'

- Chapter nineteen -

Before long, the school holidays ended and Seb, Rosa, Melody and Elise were back in the routine of school, homework, youth group and all their other activities. At first all their friends wanted to hear about their amazing holiday, but soon life settled down again.

One thing had not changed though, and that was the determination of all the family to find ways of raising money to support Kaba and his family.

The weather had begun to change, and the crisp autumn air with dewy mornings and sunny afternoons prompted Melody to enter for a 5K run, asking all her friends and family to sponsor her. After school before suppertime, she went for a training run whenever she could. Seb often joined her, taking Rix with him, because it was good exercise for them both.

The date of the run was fixed for the October half-term holiday, so Melody had plenty of time to get ready. As well as the run, she also was planning to have a piano recital in the chapel hall, and Rosa and their mum, Auntie Apple and Grandma were planning a cake stall. Ever since the success of her cherry pie, Rosa had begun to enjoy cooking, and Auntie Apple had helped her to discover a hidden talent. She was excited to show some of her school buddies how good she had become at cooking since the unfortunate incident of the fire.

Seb's Search

'I'm doing a series of paintings from my sketches in Uganda,' said Elise, when she heard about the plans. 'Maybe I could display them and see if anyone wants to buy them.'

'I know someone who will print cards from your paintings,' Mum suggested. 'Cards are always best-sellers at the hospital fête. I'll pay for the printing as my contribution.'

'Wow!' answered Elise excitedly. 'That sounds so cool. I'm sure lots of our village friends will be able to afford a card, even if they don't want any more paintings in their houses.'

Seb was proud of his sisters and their achievements but was feeling a bit despondent, thinking he had no real talent to make money for Kaba to go to school. It wasn't that he was jealous; he just felt inadequate and useless.

That evening he was very quiet, trying to think what he could do. After all, Kaba was *his* little friend. At bedtime he was still troubled, and his dad noticed how quiet he'd become.

'I think us men should have a project too,' he suggested to his son.

'I know, Dad,' Seb answered, 'but I'm no use at anything in particular like the girls are, and I can't think of anything to do.' Seb felt and looked very sad and miserable.

'Cheer up, Seb,' answered his dad. 'I've had an idea. Lots of the older folk in the village struggle at this time of the year to tidy up their gardens, pick their apples and even take their dogs out. You and I could offer our services. We can advertise in the chapel notices, local paper and the doctor's surgery. We can take the lawnmower and other tools in the trailer and do things after school and on Saturdays. There are several weeks until the end of October when the evenings are dark.'

'That's a super cool idea, Dad,' said Seb, his face brightening up. 'Perhaps some of the youth group would also help. Mr James has loads of fruit trees in his back garden, and often the apples just drop off and rot.'

'Then we could also offer a service on the day when the girls are doing their fund-raising in the chapel hall. I could hire an apple crusher and we could make apple juice for anyone who wants to use up their spare apples for a small charge,' responded his father, with a great smile. 'I've always wanted to have a go at doing that!'

'Thanks, Dad,' Seb said, now also with a huge smile. 'I was feeling so useless, but now we can do loads of things to help raise funds and also really help our neighbours.'

It was so encouraging for the family because the village folk were very enthusiastic about the project, as were many of the children's school friends and almost everyone at the chapel. Sophie was delighted to help as lots of the people already supported her cousin and knew a bit about how hard life could be for the people in rural Uganda.

The weeks until half-term just flew by with all the extra activities. It was a beautiful autumn. Seb felt as if heaven were smiling down on them as he and his dad and sometimes his school friends worked in the gardens at weekends. Seb began to really love the older folk, who were often so brave and tried to do as much as they could for themselves. Sometimes they told him

Seb's Search

stories of what it was like in the village when they were young, and he enjoyed their tales. Some of them asked if the garden service could continue all throughout the year, and his dad promised to think about that and how maybe a rota of men and boys from the church could keep it going.

The actual day of the 'Big Event', as the youngsters had dubbed the fund-raiser, was bright and sunny. Loads of people came along, far more than the Morris family had dared to dream might come, and everything went off so well. Elise was thrilled because every one of her set of twelve paintings sold as well as loads of cards.

Dad had a bright idea and auctioned the cakes, raising a lot of money. The apple pressing was also popular, and people remarked what a good idea it was. The climax of the afternoon, after everyone had eaten a lovely cream tea with Auntie Apple's wonderful home-baked scones and Grandma's strawberry jam and cream from the local farm, was Melody's piano recital.

Just before it began, she was so nervous and felt sick and was sure she wouldn't remember the notes and wished she'd never had the idea in the first place. With her tummy churning, her knees shaking and her mouth feeling dry, she opened the piano and began, but after the first few notes, her nerves disappeared as she felt the beauty of the music take over and help her to relax. The applause at the end was thunderous, and she felt very shy and shaky when she got up to take a little bow. All the family felt so proud of her!

At the end of the day, the chapel treasurer and Dad counted up the takings, and including the money that the garden project had earned, the total topped just over three thousand pounds!

There was so much cheering and clapping when the total was announced that it felt as if the roof might fall in!

The following Saturday—when Melody ran her 5K run—wasn't such a nice day, but she didn't mind. The family were cheering her on at different points in Monmouth, where the event was being held. She did well, with a new personal best, and felt elated when she crossed the finishing line. Other than running at school, it was her first official event, and the manager of the harrier club in the area came up to her and asked her is she would be willing to join their group and run regularly. Her parents promised to think about it—they didn't want their daughter to take on too much but did want to develop her talent.

When the sponsorship money was collected, she had added another £543 to the total!

That night Seb was able to face talk with Emmanuel on the internet and share the wonderful news, and then his dad arranged with George to send the money to him in Uganda to help the family and pay school fees for Kaba to go to a good school.

They also heard news from George that the trial of Kaba's father had taken place and that although he had been given a prison sentence, it was fairly lenient and he had been promised that his job would be kept for him once he had served his time.

– Chapter twenty –

After such an exciting autumn, life seemed very ordinary and dull to the family as they entered November and then December. The weather had become cold, damp and windy, and it was dark sometimes as early as three-thirty in the afternoon. Rix didn't get so many long walks, and Melody stopped running after school.

At times Seb became restless. He loved talking to Emmanuel a few times each week, but visiting Uganda hadn't really answered his questions about his birth mother. In fact, it had raised more questions than it had answered. Part of him longed to know why he was abandoned at birth, and part of him was scared to know that maybe he wasn't wanted, maybe his life was a mistake.

He had shared with the CU at school how he felt, and they had prayed with him. He tried to leave his questions with God and trust him that he had a purpose for his future, but in the dark winter days, he often found himself brooding about it.

One evening, about three weeks before Christmas during supper, the phone rang. First Mum spoke to the caller, then she called for Dad. It was unusual, and the children wondered what was going on, because they both disappeared into the snug and were talking for ages. When they returned, they looked a bit upset but didn't answer directly when Rosa asked who had phoned.

'It's nobody you would know, darling, and nothing for you to worry about,' her mum answered. 'Sorry to have been so long. The dessert is in the fridge. Can you get it please?'

Mum had that 'Don't ask me anything more' look on her face, so the kids knew it was something serious. After the meal, the girls were helping clear up, and Seb went out give Rix a short run in the garden and was surprised to see his dad follow him.

'I need to tell you about that phone call, Seb,' he explained. 'It's something for your ears alone at this point in time. It was from the social services in London, where we used to live. Apparently, a woman has come forward trying to trace you and says she is your birth mother.'

At this news, Seb felt a great surge of excitement—could he finally know the circumstances about his birth and meet his birth mother?

'Before you get too excited,' said his dad quickly, seeing his son's face, 'I need to go to London and check everything about this woman. After the kidnapping and the facts being national news in Uganda, anyone might claim to be your mother and not have good motives. For the time being, do you think you can keep the news to yourself, while we do some checks and find out if she is genuinely your birth mother? I know that's hard to ask, but I did need to talk to you before I go. How do you feel about things? Should she prove to be your mother, do you want to

Seb's Search

meet her after all these years and know her side of the story, or would you rather leave things as they are?'

Seb had often thought about this question, and he knew his answer.

'I've thought for a long time that if she were to come forward, I would like to meet her and ask her questions about why she abandoned me, and to know more about my roots. You and Mum are my real parents and always will be. Nothing can change that. I love you both to the moon and back!'

Dad and Seb had tears glistening in their eyes as they walked back to the house.

'Thanks, Seb. You are and always will be our precious son, but we are happy for you to meet this woman if she proves she is your birth mother.'

Dad went to London two days later. He had told the family that he had some business matters which needed sorting out and wasn't quite sure how long he would be away but promised to be home for the weekend.

Seb overheard the girls discussing his dad's visit when they were on the school bus. They decided that some distant relative must have died and Dad had to sort out their affairs. Seb smiled to himself—yes, a distant relative maybe, but very much alive!

He felt himself getting more and more nervous as the weekend approached, wondering what the news might be. He wanted to ask his mum if she had heard anything, but somehow he could never get her on her own, and since it was her night duty week, she wasn't around at bedtime. Auntie Apple was staying with them while Dad was away, and he doubted that she or Grandma would know the real reason why he'd gone to London.

Mum came back from work on Friday morning just as they were finishing breakfast and ready to catch the school bus.

'I chatted to Dad an hour ago as I was leaving work,' she told them, 'and he's coming home this evening, bringing a visitor for the weekend. Auntie Apple, would you mind making up the bed in the spare room for me while I get some shut-eye. I'm on nights off until Tuesday so can manage the cooking when I wake up.'

'Who's coming, Mum?' asked Rosa. 'Do we know him or her?'

'No, but that's all I'm telling you for now, so off you go and don't miss the bus!' Mum answered.

The girls chattered on about who might possibly be coming to stay for the weekend but didn't notice how quiet Seb was. He thought he knew who it could be!

– Chapter twenty-one –

'This is Nakato, Seb's birth mother,' announced Dad, when he arrived home with a tall, dark-skinned lady at his side.

'Welcome, do come in,' said Mum graciously.

The girls and Seb went to greet her. The girls were excited and smiling, but Seb was suddenly shy and unsure of what to say.

It was a day he had imagined and longed for since he was old enough to know what being adopted meant, but now he had no words. It didn't seem right to just shake hands, but it also seemed weird to hug a stranger. However, he decided to do the latter. Then he worried—what should he call her? Mum was his mum, and this lady was completely unknown to him, even if she had given birth to him.

Nakato broke the ice.

'Please call me Nakato,' she said to them all. 'I know this is a shock for you all, and I am so grateful to your father for allowing me to come and meet you. I don't want to intrude into your lives, but I am just so thrilled to see the son I gave away when he was born alive and well and in a happy family. Perhaps you will allow me to tell you my story later.'

'Of course, Nakato,' answered Seb, recovering his composure and manners. 'I'll show you to your room. Let me carry your bag.'

Seb's Search

His birth mother smiled and together they climbed the stairs as he took her to her room. Seb realised that she was as nervous and shy as he was, and somehow that helped.

'I have always wanted to know your story and to meet you,' he told her, 'and I am sure that we'll all love getting to know you. It's just been a big surprise. Dad didn't tell us that you were coming, only that he was bringing a visitor home.'

At supper the family relaxed, and Nakato learnt to recognise the differences between the triplets and call them by their correct names.

'I am one of a set of twins,' she told them. 'I have a twin brother called Wasswa. In Uganda twins are always called by certain names according to your gender and the order in which you were born, and Wasswa was born first, but I haven't seen him for years and years.'

'That's so sad,' answered Elise. 'I couldn't bear to be away from my sisters or Seb for long, even though we do argue sometimes and get on each other's nerves!'

After supper, Seb took Nakato to see the chickens while the girls helped their mum to clear the table. They knew he needed time to be alone with her.

'Did Dad tell you that we went to Uganda last August so that I could see the country you came from? We stayed at Mbarara. I'll show you my journal if you like,' he added.

'I'd love that,' Nakato answered. 'I would love to see what Mbarara looks like these days. It's been so many years since I was there,' she said sadly.

Seb's Search

'Why did you have to leave me under the bush?' Seb couldn't wait any longer to ask his birth mother.

'If you want to hear it, I'd like to tell you my story,' answered Nakato. 'It's not a good one to hear, but I hope you will understand that I loved you with all my heart and it broke my heart to leave you there. I have thought about you every day since then and said a prayer for your well-being.'

She was struggling not to cry, and Seb didn't want to embarrass her or make her feel uncomfortable in front of the family.

'Lord, help me,' he prayed silently, and then a good idea came into his mind.

'We often play games together on Friday evenings. Are you happy to do that?' he asked. 'Then tomorrow morning, if you come with me when I take Rix for his walk, you could tell me the story then.'

So that is what they did. They sat by the fire and played board games, and all ended up giggling together and having fun. Seb told everyone that he and Nakato were taking Rix for a walk after breakfast because they wanted to talk, and Mum nodded, saying that it seemed a good idea.

Fortunately Saturday was a dry morning, so Seb, Nakato and Rix set out on their walk soon after breakfast. First of all, they walked through the village.

'This is where my Grandma lives, and next door to her is Auntie Apple,' said Seb, pointing out the cottages. 'You'll meet them tomorrow if you come to chapel with us. We'll walk up

Chapel Lane and you can see the church where we go. I am a Christian and hope to be baptised soon, and so does Elise. We all belong to the youth group.'

Then they walked across the fields, and Nakato began to tell her story.

We lived just outside Mbarara in a village. My Father was a cattle keeper and was very proud of his herd of Ankole cattle. My parents already had six children when Wasswa and I were born, all of them girls! There was great rejoicing when a son was born, but I always felt left out and inferior.

The eldest of my sisters was already married, and her marriage dowry had brought more cattle wealth to my father. I so wanted to attend school and learn, but there was often not any money for my school fees and it was not thought important for girls to go to school in those days—they were only useful to help in the house and garden and then be married off. Your father chose your husband—so I knew I might be the third, fourth or fifth wife of an old man who just wanted a young girl to give him more children. It didn't sound like a good future to me!

My father had a distant cousin who had been to school and now ran a business in London. From time to time he returned to Uganda and visited his relatives. My mother had always told us girls that he was not a good man and not to be trusted. None of us knew what his business was, but he looked smart in tailored suits and leather shoes, so we knew he was prosperous.

Seb's Search

He returned to Uganda for my grandmother's funeral. All the clan had gathered, and it was a big occasion, for Grandmother was very old and much revered. I was sixteen years old and a pretty girl. This 'Uncle' Musoke seemed to like me and kept coming over to talk with me.

'What is this pretty young lady going to do with her life?' he asked me. 'Will you be a nurse, or a secretary? Why, you're so beautiful you could be a model!'

I was very flattered by his words, because all I did was help in the shamba, which was a large garden, and cook the food. And Father was already looking for a husband for me.

'Would you like to go to England and work for me?' he asked, and I couldn't believe my luck! Maybe I could be famous as a model and make a lot of money and complete my schooling in England!

Of course, I said yes, but it was the worst decision I ever made. I should have been suspicious, because he told me not to tell anyone, not even my parents or Wasswa. He took photos of me and told me he would come to the village and collect me as soon as he had acquired a passport for me. I believed Mother was wrong—he was a good man who wanted to help me have a better life.

A week or so later I was in the shamba, which is away from our house, planting sweet potatoes, and he drives up in his big Mercedes car.

'Jump in, Nakato,' he said. 'I'm taking you to Kampala. I have all your papers, and we are flying to the UK tonight.'

'But I'm dirty and in old clothes,' I remember saying. 'Let me go home and clean up first.'

'No time for that,' he said. 'I'll buy you a new dress in Kampala and everything else you need when we get to London.'

I did as I was told, and we drove off at a great speed to Kampala. I forgot my dirty clothes and felt like a queen in that Mercedes, excited about going in an aeroplane to London!

'Uncle' Musoke kept his word, and in Kampala he took me to a shop in the main street, where he bought a beautiful dress, underwear and a jacket and good shoes, ready for me to travel to the UK. I was so excited I didn't even think about going so far away without saying goodbye to my family. I felt a bit uncomfortable when he showed me how to use the shower in his apartment and watched me wash and then dress in my new clothes, but I thought of him as an uncle and never dreamt that he had evil intentions. Nobody in the family had any idea that I had been abducted and taken to the UK.

Seb and Nakato had been walking for a long time, and Rix had had a good run.

'We need to be heading back,' Seb told his birth mother. 'Everyone will be getting home for lunch. Please can you tell me the rest of the story after lunch. I'd rather hear it all from you before the family know what you went through. It must have been terrible for you.'

Seb's Search

'It was, but it was also a long time ago now. I was a very young and stupid girl, but I should have known better. All these years I have lived with regrets.'

– Chapter twenty-two –

Later that day, Seb took Nakato to his bedroom, showed her his journal from Uganda, and then took down his shoebox. Nakato gasped when she saw it.

'Mum kept it for me,' Seb told her, 'and inside are the baby clothes and your note—it has and always will be my special treasure. Can you tell me the rest of the story? I don't want you to be upset, but I want to know and understand about my birth.'

We flew to London that night, from Entebbe. I was terrified when I saw the plane and we began to climb into the skies. I was just a girl from the village with very little education and had no idea of the outside world. Even the food on the plane was weird to me, and I felt sick and scared. 'Uncle' Musoke was quite harsh and told me not to be a silly girl, that I was now going to be a working woman in London.

Life for me changed forever. I was taken to a large house in London, which my father's cousin owned. He was obviously the boss, and everyone in the house was scared of him. There were a lot of girls there and an older lady who supervised them. Many of the girls were from Uganda, and I later understood that we had all been tricked into leaving our homes and were not free to return. I won't go into any more details than that, but it was

Seb's Search

horrible. I felt so guilty, used and abused. The worst thing was that I was now a prisoner. 'Uncle' Musoke owned me like a slave.

'Auntie' Odati was not the wife of Musoke but a sort of housekeeper. She did care about us girls and had to make sure we were all ready for work every day and night, well dressed and looking beautiful for the men who visited. She was completely dominated by Musoke, who had abducted her when she had been young.

We had no pay—we were told that our food and nice clothes were more than we deserved. At first, I was just a frightened young girl, but Odati helped me to cope and I made friends with some of the girls, especially those who were from the Ankole tribe and spoke my language. We did have classes with Odoti to learn English, which we had to speak at work all the time, even though some of the visitors were Ugandan.

There was one middle-aged man who always asked for me when he came to visit the house. He was Ugandan and also came from Mbarara—he told me that, but we were not allowed to reveal any of our personal details and always, as I said before, we had to talk in English. He was polite and gentle and treated me with respect. He sometimes would bring little gifts for me and even gave me money, which I had to hide in my clothing and give to Odati, because I knew I could trust her.

I was very ignorant, and it was Auntie Odati who realised one day that I might be pregnant. Usually any girl who became pregnant would disappear for a while and didn't return with a baby, but when Auntie talked to me, whatever the consequences

I was determined to keep the baby. I told her who I thought the father was, and she talked with him and he gave her some money to look after me.

'Uncle' Musoke was furious, but I think your father was an important man and when he sided with my decision, I was given light housework to do until after your birth, on the condition that my baby was given away.

I had hardly been outside in two years, but Odati went out to shop and knew the area well. She told me the story of Moses, and how God looked after him and made him a great man, even though he had been left in the River Nile by his mother. I didn't know the Bible then, but Odati did and she used to teach me about God. She really was like a mother to me at that time. She helped me to deliver safely, then as soon as you were born found the large box, bought your baby clothes and put the box in the safest place she could find. She told me afterwards that she prayed that good people would find you and care for you. Now I know her prayers were answered.

I cried and cried after you were taken away. Musoke became angry and began to beat me, but Odati stood up to him and threatened to go to the police if he didn't stop. Every day I thought about you, and Odati and I prayed for you. After a while, things settled down and I worked, helping Odati with the housework and laundry.

The years went by and Musoke brought new young girls from time to time to work for him. I felt so sorry for them and tried to

Seb's Search

comfort and help them. From time to time a girl might run away or disappear, but we never learnt what happened to them.

Auntie Odati was my closest friend, and on Sundays she often left me in charge of the girls and slipped out to a nearby church. It was there that she learnt about the love of Jesus and one day decided to become a Christian. Her life changed and she knew that Musoke was a wicked man and she needed to go and inform the police, even if it put her life at risk.

After her testimony to the police, the house was raided and we girls were taken to a safe refuge. All of us were illegal immigrants, although some of us had lived in this country for many years. The women's refuge helped us work with the authorities to get our necessary papers or to send us back to our home countries if that was what we wanted. They also gave us counselling because of all the trauma we'd had and helped us to live in the outside world.

I had a big dilemma. I did not want to return to Uganda in shame and without even finding if my son was alive and safe. I made contact with my family, and they now know I am alive and well. As Auntie Odati had put away every little bit of money I had been given through my working life, I had enough to rent a room with her and try to find out what happened to you.'

'What happened to Musoke?' asked Seb, who was deeply moved by the story.

'He was tried and sent to prison, and he will be there for many years to come,' answered Nakato.

For a while they sat together on Seb's bed, not saying anything. Both were thinking their own thoughts. It had been a relief for Nakato to tell the story to her son, and she was grateful that he wasn't angry and didn't seem to hate her for what happened when he was born.

Seb was feeling relieved too, so glad to learn that his mother refused to abort him, that she had loved him and prayed for him all through the years, and that his father had been a kind man. He felt as if a missing piece in a jigsaw had just been found and put into place, that he was complete.

'Thank you, Nakato,' he said quietly. 'Now I understand about my birth, and that makes a huge difference for me. I adore my family—they will always be my family—but you are family too, in a different sort of way. Would it be alright if I called you Mama Nakato?' he asked.

'That would be the most wonderful name in the world to be called by,' Nakato said with tears in her eyes, 'and may I call you Ssebo? It was the only name I knew to give you.'

The pair went hand in hand down the stairs smiling, and Mum and Dad knew that all was well with their precious son Seb.

His search for identity was over.